Of Lands, Legends, & Laughter

Of Lands, Legends, & Laughter

The Search for Adventure with
NATIONAL GEOGRAPHIC

Carolyn Bennett Patterson

Fulcrum Publishing
Golden, Colorado

Library of Congress Cataloging-in-Publication Data
Patterson, Corolyn Bennett.
    Of lands, legends, and laughter: the search for adventure with National
Geographic / Carolyn Bennett Patterson.
        p.   cm.
    ISBN 1-55591-332-6
    1. Patterson, Carolyn Bennett.   2. National geographic—History.
3. Travelers—United States—Biography.   4. Women periodical editors—
United States—Biography.   5. Adventure and adventurers—United States—
Biography.   I. Title.
G69.P29A3   1998
917.304'9'092—dc21
    [b]   98-18616
                                                                         CIP

Printed in the United States of America
0   9   8   7   6   5   4   3   2   1

Fulcrum Publishing
350 Indiana Street, Suite 350 , Golden, Colorado 80401-5093
(800) 992-2908 • (303) 277-1623
website: www.fulcrum-books.com
e-mail: fulcrum@fulcrum-books.com

Table of Contents

Prologue

$\mathcal{I}$ WENT TO STRANGE LANDS, in behalf of legends and full of laughter, because travel has always been, for me, the ultimate experience—a door opening in the mind, a refreshment to the spirit, a challenge, an excitement, with moments of the purest joy.

"I travel for travel's sake," wrote Robert Louis Stevenson. "The great affair is to move." I read these words written for his classic *Travels with a Donkey in the Cévennes* as a child of twelve, growing up in Mississippi during the Great Depression. And they changed my life. Stevenson opened a window to the imagination. But it was *National Geographic* magazine that offered the magic carpet that transported me to the far corners of the earth. As the first woman editor on the magazine, responsible for the legends (or captions) that accompanied its illustrations, I traveled often and widely on writing assignments, on self-education forays, on holidays.

Despite Stevenson's announcement to the contrary, he traveled more than just "for travel's sake." He traveled for adventure: "I have been after an adventure all my life, a pure dispassionate adventure, such as befell early and heroic voyagers ... ."

In that, too, I have followed Stevenson, finding adventure in almost every aspect of life. But the greatest adventure has been in my quest for understanding the world. Through travel I have discovered that the peoples of the earth, regardless of culture, are one community, sharing a common humanity, a wonder for the mystery of life, a need for comfort and healing, and a gift for laughter. Thus, I have come to regard the odyssey of my life as an adventure into the limitless realm of the human heart.

In working for the *National Geographic* I believed that I was helping to hold a mirror before the face of that humanity, a mirror that gave the human being a better understanding of the self and other life on the planet, an understanding that could contribute to peace. It has been a source of immense personal satisfaction that I was fated through nearly thirty-seven years of tenure at the magazine to play a role in so important a mission.

CHAPTER 1

Adventure in the Early Years

Do what you can, with what you have, where you are.
—Theodore Roosevelt

I THINK OF THE PERSON of my early years as not me but Mary Carolyn, whose two given names—so much the custom in the South—could never be reduced to one, because I was named for my mother's beloved mother and her adored sister. Even when I *was* Mary-Carolyn-growing-up, another part of me often looked at her with detachment, a kind of out-of-body experience that may have been a way of avoiding pain. In a way, the consciousness that I considered the soul of me

Carolyn's childhood home in Kosciusko, Mississippi.

was always an observer, curious as to how people acted or reacted, even more curious as to what Mary Carolyn was going to say or do. It was a kind of interior journey, full of mystery and lacking recognizable landmarks. Because I knew early on that I wanted to be a writer, I viewed the split in my conscious self as a potentially useful tool that would give me a clear-eyed assessment of the world.

Although my family moved from Kosciusko, Mississippi, to Jackson when I was a toddler, and we lived four years in Yazoo City, Mississippi, I considered Kosciusko my hometown, situated on the historic Natchez Trace and named after Thadeusz Kosciuszko, the Polish patriot who fought on our side during the American Revolution. Family tradition held that an ancestor served with Kosciuszko during the battle at Saratoga, New York, and when that ancestor later settled in the Mississippi Territory he named the village he helped to establish after his admired comrade-in-arms. Although the story may have had no basis in fact, I wanted to believe it because I felt the need to be in tune with famous men, great events, stirring times, and romantic causes. Such feelings, I believed, enriched the true home of my imagination.

The town of Kosciusko—tucked into the red clay hills of central Mississippi—was a place of staggering poverty during the Depression. My father, James H. Bennett, was a bookkeeper at the local feed and flour mill and cheerfully did the work of three men for a meager, subsistence wage. A man of even temper with a sense of humor, a lover of books and music, and an elder in the First Presbyterian Church, my father had once hoped to be a writer but hard times had beaten that ambition out of him. By the time his only daughter became old enough to know him as a person, he was chained to his bookkeeping desk for up to 15 hours a day, enslaved by the only ambition left to him: to provide for his family.

My mother, Nola Lansdale Bennett, was born in Kosciusko, a part of the gentry, and it was her comfortable childhood home, only a block from the town square, that sheltered the family. A graduate in music from Blue Mountain College, a Baptist woman's college in northern Mississippi, she could get no work in her profession as a piano teacher and, as a consequence, took jobs on various projects funded by the Works Project Administration, including one that helped establish the first library in the town. Sensitive and proud, with real executive ability, Nola worked outside her home because the family sorely needed the money, but she considered such work beneath her and never understood her daughter's desire to enter the business world, to be something more than a homemaker.

My brother Jim, my only sibling and four years my elder, worked at whatever odd jobs he could find. Mostly, though, he played music, first the piano, taught by our mother, then the trombone, which became the love of his life. It was the trombone, which he played in a series of dance bands, that bought him a college education in engineering and later helped pay for my college tuition.

Carolyn with her father James H. Bennett, her mother Nola Lansdale Bennett, and her brother James Jr.

As a kid growing up in Kosciusko, I was deeply aware of the Depression, of the different status of the blacks, and of the love given me by my father, mother, and brother. There was so little extra money in the family that college for my brother proved a real challenge, prompting a family conference. By his skill at playing the trombone, he had won a band scholarship to Holmes Junior College in nearby Goodman, Mississippi. The question raised at our conference: Could we cut spending enough to raise the $5 a week needed to feed my brother at college? Yes, it was decided, and from that time onward I had little interest in money or what it could buy. Moreover, I tried to talk my mother out of buying anything for me, even a remnant of material for a dress. Today I treasure a quilt sewn by my mother, featuring butterflies fashioned from scraps of material left over from those little homemade dresses, bought by so much sacrifice.

As for the treatment of blacks, I learned compassion and caring for them from my parents. My father, who was the paymaster at the flour mill, counted a number of the black workers there among his friends. He also thought a number of them were like children, because every Sunday morning, following Friday pay-day and Saturday play day, several black men would come to call, to borrow money against next week's wages. I could hear my father lecturing them about their responsibilities to wives and children, the evils of drinking and gambling, the dangers of debt. And, all the while, he would be getting out the money the men wanted—as, of course, they knew he would.

My mother had a black male friend, our plumber Mr. Sam. He and she shared a love for trees and flowers and had long conversations about how best to produce the finest roses or to encourage a sapling to grow. They would exchange cuttings from their prized plants and compare notes as to the success of such endeavors. One day I came upon the two with arms around one another and both crying. It seems that the town had cut down several huge oak trees that bordered Mr. Sam's sidewalk in order to widen the street. (We had similar venerable oaks lining our sidewalk.) Mr. Sam loved those trees and was devastated. My mother shared in his sorrow and was trying to comfort him. Mr. Sam's race held no bar to their friendship.

Kosciusko was so small in those days—about 1,700 people—that everyone knew everyone else and most families were linked by blood or marriage. Kinship was important, and fourth, fifth, and sixth cousins were considered family. It was at the town cemetery, set atop a hill with a commanding view of the countryside, tree-greened in summer, that I studied my family tree at my mother's side and learned the burden of her heritage.

I can see myself now, ready to enter high school in the fall of 1934, reed-thin with long black curly hair, walking with mother to the cemetery, carrying a bunch of flowers from the yard to put on the family graves. We go on Saturday afternoon because we want the graves to look their best when most of the visitors come out on Sunday.

"Your grandmother would have loved these mums," Nola says, pulling weeds from the grass covering her mother's grave.

---

*"She worked so hard in her life she never had the time she would
have liked to spend with flowers," Nola grieved, tears falling.
"But she did it all for me and my sisters. Our parents sent all
three of us to college at a time girls just didn't get a higher
education. I remember her saying, 'Papa and I want you girls to
have a good education so you can make something of yourselves.'
And look," says Nola, reproaching herself, "what little we have
done with our lives ... if it weren't for you children ... ."*

*Nola pauses and looks thoughtfully at me. "My grand-
mother," she says, waving toward her grandmother's grave, "did
the same for my mother, going without so that SHE could have
things. And, of course, your father and I are doing our very best
by you children."*

Awash with guilt, I give my mother a hug.

Out of remembrance of those hours at the cemetery, out of the
poverty that prevailed, came the birth of a resolution: I would pay
the debt to those earlier generations and make it in the world
myself. Furthermore, I would break the chain of responsibility to
ancestors and not pass on to my children the burden of their ambi-
tions. And, like Scarlet O'Hara, shaking her fist and crying "As
God is my witness," I would never be poor again.

It was at the height of the struggle to survive in 1933 that the
Bennett family had moved from Yazoo City back to Nola's family
home in Kosciusko. Making a living in Yazoo City had been hard
and finally impossible, but the town itself, situated on the edge of
the Mississippi Delta, treasured amenities that gave a lift to life,
especially for me. There were streets lined with huge handsome old
homes with white columns outside and antiques within. The Episco-
pal Church was the leading religious institution. There was a country
club with a swimming pool, golf course, and tennis courts. There
were dances at the club on Saturday nights, for kids as well as grown-
ups. My family didn't belong to the club, but I was often invited to it
by friends. And though I and others my age dated—and exchanged
an occasional tentative kiss—sex played little or no part in the scene.

The move to Kosciusko was a culture shock. Gone was the Delta belief that life was to be enjoyed, even if it kept one in debt at the bank. In its place was the Puritan ethic that decreed hard work the prime virtue and debt a disgrace. Gone was Yazoo's country club with swimming, dancing, and games. In Kosciusko, there was no country club, no swimming pool, no golf course, and there was only one private tennis court. Fundamentalist intolerance replaced Episcopalian urbanity. In Kosciusko, dancing, card playing, and mixed bathing (males and females swimming together) were decreed a sin, along with kissing, petting, and other related sexual activities. And, because the young people of Kosciusko were denied regular games, with churchgoing the only sanctioned social activity, they did play at sex, sinful though it might have been.

I was the most popular girl in town that first summer after moving from Yazoo City—until the boys who plied me with sexual advances discovered me to be less than receptive. Perhaps I was too young, too romantic, too hard to please, or maybe too frightened. Perhaps the fun and real games of Yazoo City had spoiled me. But after that brief, ephemeral popularity, no boy asked me on a date until I was in college. And I set out as a loner on a journey inward.

That journey may have its beginning in the heat-blistered summer of 1934 when the thunder comes from the First Baptist Church, whose red-brick, white-columned sanctuary crowns a hill on Jackson Street, within sight of the Bennett home. Except for Jim, who is in his room endlessly trying to duplicate on his trombone Tommy Dorsey's version of "Sentimental over You," the family is gathered on the front porch. It is Saturday night, the one night of the week that James Bennett spared himself extra labor at the office. And supper—cold biscuits, ham, and jam—is over.

"It's a big night tonight, up at the church," says my father, rocking in his chair. "Tonight's the last night of the revival and

*the visiting preacher can count up how many souls he's saved."
Dad laughs; he is a believer but has been heard to express the
forthright opinion that many things about religion are "non-
sense," especially when people get "wrought-up" and things "get
out of hand."*

*All week long mother and I have sat on the porch, gently
swinging to and fro in the glider to stir a breath of air and
listening to the shouting and singing coming from the church. It
is no different this evening. Even my brother's trombone playing
is faint in contrast to the thunderous voice of the Baptist
preacher, begging, berating, damning, pleading, exhorting,
cajoling, threatening: "Come to Christ! Come to Christ! You live
lives of sin and have angered God. He will send you to hell to
burn forever. Give your heart to the Master. He offers you
salvation from the eternal flames. Time is short. Come, let the
world know you have been born again and are a Christian."*

*"I think I'll go up to the church and see what's going on," I
tell my parents.*

*"OK, baby," says my father. "We'll watch you walk over.
Don't be too late coming home."*

*My parents follow with their eyes the slight figure as I cross
the street, climb the high flight of stairs to the entrance of the
church, and go inside.*

*The heat in the church is staggering as I slip into a seat at
the very back. The congregation is now singing "Just as I Am,"
as the minister is pleading. "Come, come, come to Christ. Won't
you come? He is calling, calling to you. Come now to the front
of this sanctuary and tell the world that you are born again—a
Christian."*

*Women in housedresses, men in shirtsleeves, their offspring
lined up beside them in the pews, some singing, some crying,
some moaning, some shouting, some on their feet marching
resolutely down the aisle to the front of the church, some already
at the front, hugging and kissing, being hugged and kissed, the*

*shine of sweat on their faces. "Glory be to God!" shouts the
minister.*

*A wave of nausea sweeps over me and I slip outside and run
home. Whatever God was in the church, I didn't want to know.
But the raw emotion and the manipulation of raw emotion that
I had seen frightens me, and I sleep fitfully.*

*The next morning I am up at dawn and, still in my night-
dress, go out to the front porch where the coolness comes as a
blessing. Sitting in the swing, watching as the early sun sends
shafts of light, as from heaven, down through the huge oak trees
in the yard, I am suffused by a sense of peace so comforting, so
healing, so beautiful that I think it must come from God—some
God from somewhere. Suddenly I feel safe, cared for, perhaps
loved by something beyond my understanding. Maybe I had
found a friend for the journey to my inner world.*

I never have resolved in my mind if I had had what is called a
"religious experience." But what had happened that summer morning, ever fresh in memory throughout my life, gave me confidence,
optimism, freedom from fear. Throughout the globe-ranging travels of my adult years, nothing ever seemed truly life threatening.
The world, as it were, wore a smiling face.

There were globe-ranging travels in those teen years too, but
they all occurred vicariously through the pages of books and magazines—and in my vivid imagination. My father's love of books
had brought into the home a complete set of Redpath's *History of
the World,* big, heavy volumes illustrated with romanticized drawings of faraway places and long-ago times. And there was the Bible,
of course. I was enchanted with the beauty and cadences of the
King James Version and committed whole chapters to memory.
My father subscribed to the national weekly newspaper *Grit* and
Holland's Magazine of the South. I read everything from cover to
cover and read Redpath and the Bible many times.

I read straight through the high school library. Then, in the
years before the town library got started, I began searching for

books in private collections. In the meanwhile, I started composing books of my own by talking rather than writing them out. At the same time, I would play tennis with myself, bouncing a ball against the side of the house.

One of the longest—and most memorable—of my books was called "Clouds Without Water," from a quotation in the Bible, "Be not like clouds without water, full of wind, signifying nothing." It was packed with the kind of action I had never seen and the kind of people I had never met. Another of my novels, called "Visiting the Sins of the Father," a title also taken from the Bible, was a tragedy covering a century in the life of a wicked family.

When I was twelve, my father, through some sacrifice or other, bought me a new portable typewriter, which I taught myself to use. "Now, baby," he admonished, "write about something you know. Look around you. Write about something you see." And I started writing a novel laid in deepest Africa, with descriptions of animals I knew only from their pictures and tribal customs I made up in my head. The call to excitement was too strong. Kosciusko— the familiar—was too tame to compete. But the daily, hours-long practice in using words, often with a King James Version ring to them, had begun. Before I knew it, I had fallen in love with the English language.

And I had fallen in love with travel. Reading Robert Louis Stevenson's *Travels with a Donkey in the Cévennes* I learned that I wanted to be a writer who traveled, and I wanted to retrace his journey through the mountains of southern France with a donkey as a companion. Moreover, I started training for it early, striking out from home for long solitary walks in the nearby hills, fields, and woods.

There was no donkey to accompany me, but, like Stevenson, I sharpened my powers of observation and developed language skills by confiding, through a period of several years, in a kind of oral journal, one that I kept by speaking aloud as I strolled down farm lanes and woodland paths. I found the purest pleasure in the sound of certain words and repeated them over and over, just for the joy of it. I must have been the object of unease, casting doubt as to my mental and emotional health. Think of it: a slender, sloe-eyed girl—at the beginning only twelve years old, then a teenager—ranging the countryside alone, speaking continuously and sometimes shouting out particularly wonderful words.

On a childhood visit to cousins in Memphis, Tennessee, I "discovered" the Mississippi River, whose sweep, power, and muddy grandeur inspired in me a wild excitement. Father of Waters is what people called the Mississippi. But for me it was the Mother of Dreams. I yearned to follow the river to the sea and then to board a boat to sail across that sea, and another sea, and all the seas on earth.

I am a junior in high school when THE TRIP comes up. As a flute player in the Kosciusko High School Band, I will accompany the band to Forth Worth, Texas, where my high school football team is to play a Fort Worth team. It is 1936, the year Texas celebrates the centennial of its declaration of independence from Mexico.

Weeks of research precede the trip but material on Texas is scarce. When the Holland's Magazine of the South *arrived at my home, I quickly find a treasure. The magazine carries a story on the Fort Worth Botanical Gardens. In one picture, a gracious white colonnade dominates a small hill overlooking a profusion of exotic trees and flowers. Looking at the scene I think I have never seen anything so exquisite. The columns put Greece in mind. The pine trees look like Australia; the flowers are look-alikes of those in the jungles of South America. And I marvel that I am going to be lucky enough to see it with my own eyes.*

The band travels by train to Fort Worth and arrives just in time to be transported by bus to the high school stadium where the night football game is to be played. It is pouring rain. The band sits huddled under raincoats, making music at intervals. At halftime we pour onto the field to spell out in marching maneu-

vers "F W" for Fort Worth, and play "The Eyes of Texas." It is cold, near freezing, and after the halftime misery sets in. At the end of the game, we Kosciusko kids literally stagger out of the stadium and into the nearby gym where the Fort Worth High School Band has invited us for refreshments.

It is nearing midnight when, now thawed out, I find myself with young people willing to drive me to the Fort Worth Botanical Gardens. With freezing rain still falling, the group arrives at the white colonnade. Peering into the gloom, I am speechless with the wonder of it all, seeing, on my own, a famous place, one made even more famous by a magazine article just published. I am experiencing a touch of Greece, Australia, and South America. I am a traveler.

As a graduation present from high school, my mother arranged another trip for me. She wrote an old college friend who lived in Gulfport, Mississippi, and asked if it would be possible for me to visit her for a week. I had never seen the sea; it would be a special treat.

I traveled to the Mississippi Gulf coast by bus, but it was not until my hostess took me in her car that I caught my first sight of the Gulf of Mexico. The heart-catching, terrifying beauty of the sea, stretching to awesome infinity, the very embodiment of boundless freedom, caught me in a lifelong embrace. And I burst into tears—tears of happiness—for I felt at home, by the sea, at last.

CHAPTER 2
Adventure in Growing Up

We judge ourselves by what we feel capable of doing,
while others judge us by what we have already done.
— Henry Wadsworth Longfellow

LEAVING KOSCIUSKO BEHIND, I set sail for college on another voyage of self-discovery. For my first college year, I decided to follow in my mother's footsteps and go to Blue Mountain College, whose president, Dr. Lawrence Lowrey, was her longtime friend. With a student body of about 300, the college was set in a small village in northern Mississippi whose single drugstore constituted "downtown."

Deeply religious, of southern Baptist persuasion and all female at that time, the college forbade dancing, card playing, smoking, drinking, and anything more intimate than hand-holding on a date, which for first-year students was limited to once a week, on campus only. All offenses were punishable by expulsion. Working my way through college as a library assistant, dining room waitress, kitchen helper, and gofer for the college's public relations officer, I still found time to sell advertising space for the college yearbook *Mountain Breeze,* play the flute in the college orchestra, and prowl country lanes "writing" my books out loud. And I found, for the first time outside my parent's home, the encouragement to pursue life as a writer. It came from my English teacher, Mrs. Cox, who also taught me how to spell correctly. Since her students got an automatic "F" on any paper turned in with a misspelled word, I quickly learned the uses of a dictionary.

I loved Blue Mountain but left to go to Mississippi State College (now University) for my second year, believing, correctly, that I needed a broader experience to prepare me for journalism school at the University of Missouri, one of the three best in the United States at the time. During that first week at Mississippi State—with an enrollment of 5,000 men and 500 women—I played a game of bridge at the school's YMCA. Not knowing that the stakes were for money, I lost the cash for my weekly meal ticket. That captured my attention and, thereafter, my game so improved that I made enough money at bridge to feed myself for the two semesters I spent there. I also worked in the registrar's office for Mr. Ben Hilburn, later college president, who assigned me the job of ferreting out those students suffering from malnutrition due to lack of money for meal tickets. For extracurriculars, I worked on the school newspaper, played in Mississippi State's famous Maroon Band (whose president and manager, Joe Thompson, became a lifelong friend), and served as president of the International Relations Club, presiding over meetings that attracted the attendance of Sonny Montgomery, a thirty-year veteran of the U.S. House of Representatives.

When traveling to the University of Missouri and its school of journalism for my junior year, something happened that to this day remains vivid in my memory. I rode a segregated bus to St. Louis, Missouri. Then, for the trip to Columbia, Missouri, the university's town, I boarded a bus that was nonsegregated, taking a window seat in the forward section with the aisle seat vacant. Just before the bus pulled out of the station, a well-dressed, middle-aged black woman came aboard and took the aisle seat next to me.

Facing a situation I had never encountered before, I was caught in an agony of indecision. What should I do? Remain where I was and feel uncomfortable or move and risk hurting my seatmate's feelings? In the end, I moved, to a seat in the back of the bus. I hated myself for it, but the incident taught me something valuable: that prejudice is insidious and can catch one unaware. Although I had never been taught prejudice at home, the incident proved that my conscience was intact and that I knew right from wrong. The racial prejudice of the society I had known all my life had no hold on my mind and heart.

I had joined the Chi Omega Fraternity (read Sorority) at Mississippi State, using money I made as a carhop at an ice cream parlor in Kosciusko. My wage at the time: 24 cents an hour. And so, at the University of Missouri, I went to live in the Chi Omega house with a bunch of young women who struck me as snobs. There was a house rule, for example, forbidding Chi Omegas to date Jews. This in the fall of 1940 when the persecution of the Jews by the Nazis was at its height and abhorred by the civilized world! I broke the rule whenever a Jewish boy asked me for a

date. Another hard-to-take fact: Missouri was a hard-drinking school, proud of its reputation as the "country club of the Midwest," and I had come from a teetotaling family and town. Finding it hard to adjust, I began having migraine headaches. I was absent from so many classes that the journalism school dean called me in on one occasion and announced that I had missed more classes while maintaining passing grades than any student known to have attended the school. I left Missouri after one semester, making up the lost credits by going to Mississippi State during the summer of 1941.

At Louisiana State University I found the college of my dreams. I immediately began working for *The Daily Reveille,* the tabloid-size college newspaper, and was shortly named one of its five campus editors. My teachers in the school of journalism became my friends as did many of the university's student leaders whose activities

A senior at Louisiana State University, standing beneath the university tower.

I covered as a reporter-editor. Three of my Chi Omega sisters—Wink Dameron, president of the sorority; Che Che Hinkle, member of the student council and an outstanding transfer student; and Jewel Claitor, editor of *The Daily Reveille*—became my best friends for life, and we continue to have reunions every year.

Dr. Robert Heilman, the distinguished essayist, taught me English literature and introduced me to his colleagues on the faculty, the poet Cleanth Brooks and the novelist Robert Penn Warren, whose novel about the regime of Louisiana's Governor Huey Long, *All the King's Men,* made him famous. I thought of those L.S.U. professors as the Three Stars. And when I subsequently became editor of *The Summer Reveille,* the Stars fed me ideas for editorials calling for improvements in the life of the university. Louisiana State University's

Campus editor of The Daily Reveille, *L.S.U.*

President General Luther B. Hodges invited me for breakfast once a week to discuss what I might be writing an editorial about, hoping to forestall any criticism of his administration. The night before my breakfast meeting with President Hodges, the Three Stars would meet and decide what needed fixing, passing the word on to me. Almost invariably, President Hodges would order a fix *before* the paper went to press, making an editorial superfluous. It may not have been good journalism but the end result was a happy one. (After I moved to Washington, D.C., following World War II, Dr. Heilman visited me every year when he came to the nation's capital as a member of the Phi Beta Kappa Senate. And, years later, following a speech I made at Yale University, Dr. Brooks, then a professor there, came to dine with me at the table of the provost of Pierson College.)

But the overpowering news of my year at L.S.U. was the attack on Pearl Harbor and the outbreak of World War II. The word came to me at a fraternity picnic. I organized a campus demonstration with my friends, beating a drum on the lead car of the parade, calling students to gather at President Hodges's home. There the president urged us to remain calm. "You'll all have a chance to serve your country," he said. And most of us did.

Having eschewed physical education during four years of changing colleges, I discovered that L.S.U. would not graduate me in the spring of 1942 without completing two credits in, yes, physical education. So I had to stay on for the summer, taking creative dance, swimming, golf, and tennis. I also worked at *The Summer Reveille* and served as campus correspondent for the *New Orleans States*. Upon graduating from L.S.U. that summer, President Hodges invited my parents as his houseguests. The graduation ceremony was on Saturday. The following Monday I reported to work at my new job as a general news reporter for the *New Orleans States*.

Season's Greetings

From The Owl's Nest
Wink Che Che Bennett Jewel

On the balcony of the Owl's Nest in the New Orleans French Quarter, overlooking the spire of St. Louis Cathedral in 1942: (from left) Wink Dameron, Che Che Hinkle, Carolyn (called Bennett by college friends), and Jewel Claitor.

My sorority sisters, Wink, Che Che, and Jewel, had preceded me to the city following their graduation in the spring, and I joined them to share a single basement room in the elegant St. Charles Avenue Boarding House, owned and run by the mother of Chep Morrison, who later became mayor of New Orleans. In a couple of months we moved to our own apartment on Orleans Street in the French Quarter, with a balcony overlooking the Royal Street garden of the St. Louis Cathedral. We called it "The Owl's Nest," after the mystical bird of Chi Omega.

In almost no time at all, I felt like I *owned* New Orleans. With many of its male reporters going off to war, the *States* gave me a wide variety of beats: the first female police reporter; ships' news reporter; fire truck chaser; hotel reporter; music, art, and nightclub critic; and reporter of general news, the job for which I was hired.

In my police reporting, I was obliged to cover the crimes committed by the Mafia. In the middle of one night in 1943, the police called me at home to tell me that a French Market butcher had his head chopped off on his own butcher's block and to ask if I would like to come survey the scene. I quickly dressed and walked the three blocks from the apartment to the French Market. It took but a glance to take in the horror of the grisly scene and remember it for life. The police told me the name of a possible witness to the murder, which they believed had been committed by the Mafia because the butcher was not willing to pay for Mafia protection. The witness lived in the French Quarter, within walking distance, so I went over for an interview. He was a living, quivering picture of fear, leaving no doubt as to what he had seen. The next day, the witness disappeared and his body was found a few weeks later in a lime pit on the Mafia-owned property of a roadhouse where I had partied with newspaper friends the night before the discovery.

On the days I covered the police, I went to work at 4 A.M. at the press room of the Criminal Courts Building. Shortly thereafter, I would attend the lineup of suspicious people the police had picked up throughout the night. As the only woman—there were no female detectives at the time—and the only member of the press present, I would sit in the back of the room and out of the vision of most of the men, who resented me. One morning, as several suspects were lined up on the lighted stage, one of the detectives shouted "That looks like the black man who raped a white woman in Little Rock!" whereupon several burly detectives leaped onto the stage and started beating the suspect. The scene became so violent and bloody that I became sick to my stomach and started vomiting. My upset called attention to me and the beating stopped, leaving the victim lying motionless on the stage. When I returned to the pressroom, the chief of detectives came to call. "The boys just got a little out of hand," he explained, adding that the beaten man was being taken to Charity Hospital for treatment.

I rushed back to the office and told my city editor that I was going to Charity Hospital to get the black man's side of the story, to which he replied, "The paper won't print his story. So forget it, Bennett."

"But the man has been tried by no court of law," I countered. "He may be guilty but that doesn't give the detectives the right to half kill him." My words fell on deaf ears so I stormed out, heading for Charity Hospital. When I arrived at the emergency room I was told that the man was dead, "shot while trying to escape."

Carolyn with city editor Frank Allen at the New Orleans States *in 1942.*

As real battles raged across Europe, Africa, and the Pacific, I was sent to cover the War of Plaquemine Parish, which pitted the forces of parish boss, Leander Perez, against his political opponent, the governor of Louisiana. The sheriff of the parish, a Perez creature, died and the governor appointed his own man. Perez called out his own militia to prevent the new appointee from taking office. The governor called out the state National Guard. As they faced one another in a standoff on the highway leading to the parish, I was sent with a photographer to the parish seat, which boasted no more than a courthouse and a general store. We lived for two days and a night out of the office car, eating from cans bought from the general store and watching what might develop. Finally, Perez had his men load the files of the sheriff's office onto a Mississippi River barge, and they sailed away. The governor's man took office in a headquarters bare of records. Back in New Orleans, I went around to Perez's office to interview him. He became so incensed at my questions that he literally kicked me out of his office, sending me sprawling on the floor of an outside corridor.

My hotel beat was considerably more pleasurable than covering politics. At the St. Charles Hotel, I interviewed Captain Eddy Rickenbacker of World War I fame as well as movie star William Holden, newly commissioned as an officer in the navy. I learned of the secret visit of President Franklin Roosevelt but, alas, was not permitted to interview him. On my ships' beat I interviewed the officers and men on a hospital ship bound for the beach at Anzio, the Allied port used for the invasion of Italy—and briefly considered stowing away, so anxious was I to get into the war.

CHAPTER 3

Adventure in Becoming

You always pass failure on the way to success.
—Mickey Rooney

WHILE WAITING TO BE CALLED UP BY THE RED CROSS, I went to New York City and lived for two months with a friend of a friend in Greenwich Village. My hostess, Essie Carlson, introduced me to a number of her friends—writers, actors, dancers, and artists. We all met frequently in someone's apartment to show off our various talents. Writers would read from their latest work, actors would perform a scene from a hope-to-play-someday play, and dancers would dance.

There was one black man in the group who struck me as the most talented writer among us. But when we would all walk arm in arm across Washington Square he was always at the other end of the line from me, and when we would meet in someone's apartment, he was always across the room from me. Finally I asked him if I had done something to offend him.

"Carolyn," he answered, "I know you are from the Deep South, and you may never have been with a black man in a social situation. I just wanted you to have a chance to get used to me and, maybe, like me simply as a person." The man's name was James Baldwin, who in just a few years would become an acclaimed writer. For many years thereafter I wanted to write up the incident and send it to *Readers Digest* for consideration in the magazine's feature, "The most memorable person I ever met." But, alas, I never did.

When I was finally called up by the Red Cross and posted to my job as a recreational assistant at the Army Redistribution Station #2 in Miami Beach, Florida, I met U.S. airmen who had completed—and survived—their missions in Europe and were sent for some recreation time before reassignment. If married, their wives came with them; if single, we recruited young women in the area to come to the beach and play with the men. The average stay was two weeks and the job of the Red Cross women was to fill that time with every imaginable kind of party. We gave dances, beach parties, deep-sea fishing parties, horse-racing parties, horseback-riding parties, nightclub parties, jai alai parties. I taught bridge and gave bridge parties.

My hotel on Collins Avenue was called the Monroe Towers, and it served enlisted Air Force men and noncommissioned officers. I had a desk in the lobby where I could see everything going on. One morning I saw a new face behind the

Carolyn as a recreational assistant for the American Red Cross at the U.S. Army Air Force Redistribution Station No. 2 in Miami Beach, Florida, during World War II.

hotel's front desk. He was, without any doubt, the most handsome man I had ever seen—something of a cross between Gregory Peck and Abraham Lincoln. So I sailed over and exclaimed to the newcomer, "I'm Carolyn Bennett of the American Red Cross. I do hope we shall be friends!"

I was given a long, cool look. Then came the reply, "Who the hell cares?" Instantly, I was hooked but it took Frederick Gillis "Pat" Patterson a good three days before he discovered that he was in love with me too. In time he got around to explaining how his four years of army life, including time on the remote Galapagos Islands guarding the Panama Canal against Japanese attack, had made him leery of what might appear to be a good thing such as his job as manager of my hotel, assigned to him with no training or experience.

At war's end, Pat and I were married in a candlelight service in Kosciusko's First Presbyterian Church, and after a brief interlude back in New Orleans and L.S.U., he and I set off for Washington, D.C., to seek our fortune. Our total capital: 80 borrowed bucks. But where New Orleans had given me every opportunity to practice my newspaper profession, Washington at first gave me none at all, since the men and women who served in the armed forces came home from military service and returned to former jobs—as promised by the government—or, as veterans, got first crack at new employment opportunities. And so I began a four-year search for a permanent job.

Of course, there were some temporary jobs. I briefly served as an editor for the Office of Scientific Research and Development, a wartime agency in its final days, putting commas, periods, conjunctions, and prepositions into research papers. For a time, I was the Washington representative for a New York public relations firm handling musical artists such as Enzio Pinzo, Patrice Munzell, and Lily Pons—great concert stars in their day. I also worked as a stringer for the *Cleveland News* covering Capitol Hill for an agency whose most frequent challenge was meeting the payroll.

At some point I met the Washington newsman and Civil War historian Scott Hart, who was then working for *Kiplinger Newsletter*. Scott wanted to help, and though he couldn't offer any kind of position at *Kiplinger,* he did have some good advice: "Try to get on at the *National Geographic* magazine, Carolyn. Take anything available, even a job scrubbing floors. Anything to get you in the door. After that you can work your way up."

The *National Geographic!* The name alone gave me a thrill. It was another way of saying "travel," "adventure." To aspire to work for the *National Geographic* magazine was to aspire to start at the top. It was in a class by itself, far above all other magazines. The National Geographic Society, the world's largest nonprofit, scientific, and educational institution with a phenomenal membership of 1,400,000 in 1949, published the *National Geographic* magazine as its official journal. The publication then, as it has always been, was printed on quality paper, full of spectacular color photographs, with a cover distinctively trimmed in yellow.

Scott Hart gave me the name of a *Geographic* writer who was his friend, Bill Nicholas, and suggested I call him. "Come on around now," said Nicholas when I got him on the phone. "I'm going to Switzerland in the morning."

Our interview was a stand-up one in the elegant, marble-floored reception hall of the National Geographic Society Headquarters on 16th Street. Nicholas was slender and quick-moving, with the kind of good looks that dissipation makes romantic. He was a man of immense charm, and he knew it. He liked people and made an effort with them. When he discovered that I came from Mississippi, he told me he had just finished a story for *National Geographic* on Natchez, Mississippi, and it was a pleasure just to meet another person from Mississippi.

We talked about his upcoming trip to Switzerland, which I thought was wildly exciting. To be a writer sent to Europe on a story struck me as the pinnacle of achievement. And, in fact, in 1949, before the great worldwide explosion of tourism, a trip to peacetime Europe really was newsworthy.

"Tell you what," Nicholas said briskly, as if we were fellow conspirators, "you come and see me when I get back from Switzerland, in about three months, and we can talk some more." Three months. An eternity. I had met a star of the famous *National Geographic* magazine. He wanted to talk to me some more. How could I wait?

But once out of the magnetic presence of Mr. William H. Nicholas, reality bore down. Nothing had been offered; I still had no job or any real prospect of one. My brief brush with Nicholas and the perceived glamour of his life made me feel more left out than ever. The world was passing me by, I grieved, with the absolute conviction of youth.

"Why don't you go down to Mississippi and visit your folks," Pat suggested, seeing that gloom had settled in. And in Mississippi I did discover something cheering: a new bronze Studebaker convertible with real leather seats. My father loaned me the down payment and I assumed the obligation to pay $82 monthly for two years. I drove it back to Washington as a surprise for Pat. A fiscal conservative, he was shocked. We had had no car because we couldn't afford one on his Library of Congress salary. I still didn't have a job.

"I'll take any kind of work to get the money for the payments," I said to Pat reassuringly. "Just having the car gives me a lift. You'll see, life will be better." I began daily searching the "Help Wanted" ads in *The Washington Post*. Then, one day, I found it: "Wanted: File clerks at the National Geographic Society's Eckington facility. Apply Personnel Department, Eckington." And I remembered Scott Hart's advice: "Take anything. Even scrubbing floors."

The Eckington facility, situated in northeast Washington, was a large warehouse of a building near Judd and Detweiler, the *Geographic*'s printer, and the railroad tracks over which rolled the magazine's monthly editions. Eckington kept the records of the Society's awesome membership.

In those years the personnel office, serving both Headquarters and Eckington, was headed by Miss Mable Strider, who did all the hiring for the Society herself. A small muscular woman with a masculine haircut, Miss Strider was perfectly named since her walk was literally a stride. After I had completed my application form and she had a chance to look it over, Miss Strider strode out of her office to greet me. She invited me to come in.

"You have an interesting application, Mrs. Patterson," she began, "but you are overqualified for work as a file clerk. Your university degree, your years as a newspaper reporter. You wouldn't be satisfied just filing cards."

"Yes, Miss Strider, I know I am overqualified," I said quickly, "but believe me, I will do a good job for you. And I really need the money. You see, I bought this car ... ."

Miss Strider interrupted. "You are overqualified to be a file clerk, but we have been looking for someone with just your qualifications for two years to work in our editorial department at Headquarters. The job would pay twice the salary we could offer you as a file clerk ... ."

At that point I must have slipped away mentally, lost in some wild, unheard rejoicing because, though Miss Strider talked on and on, I never heard what job she was offering. All I knew was: Yes, yes, yes, I would take it. She told me—and I did hear this—to report to the Geographic's library at Headquarters at 8:30 A.M. on October 3, 1949.

Librarian Miss Esther Ann Manion, a birdlike woman of formidable intelligence and sweet manner, was quite adamant. "You do not work for me, Mrs. Patterson. You are not on the library staff. Of course, you are welcome to read here, that is what the library is all about. Do familiarize yourself with our stacks."

The Geographic's library, perhaps the finest in the world devoted to geography, is open to the public as part of the Society's mission to increase and diffuse geographic knowledge, as called for in its charter. In those days, the library occupied Hubbard Hall, the Society's first home of its own, a small jewel-like building on the southwest corner of 16th and M Streets, NW. The library's public reading room was on the second floor, reached by a curving double staircase of marble and decorated with paintings by Nathaniel Wyeth, patriarch of the famous family of artists. The room itself was two stories high with a huge marble fireplace at one end and long French windows facing 16th Street.

It was hard for me to believe that one minute I could be pounding the streets, jobless, and the next minute ensconced amid elegance and beauty in the National Geographic Society library. But what was I ensconced *doing?* That was the troubling question.

Since no one had come along to claim me, I tried to look busy and did, in fact, keep busy—reading the *National Geographic* magazine. Years later, in speeches to journalism classes, I would emphasize time and again the enormous value of knowing every-thing possible about the publication one wants to write for. And those early days in the library provided me with a golden oppor-tunity. I simply read on and on and on. All the while, however, I was growing increasingly uneasy.

"How are you doing, Mrs. Patterson?" Miss Strider inquired on a chance encounter in the hall one day. And quickly I responded: "Fine, just fine, Miss Strider. Thank you." What could it all mean? I wondered. Had she made a mistake in hiring me? Who did I work for? I tried to remember our first meeting. What had Miss Strider said that I hadn't heard?

Slowly the conviction grew that I had been stationed in the library to do just what I was doing: to read the magazine and, perhaps, to offer suggestions as to what stories the magazine would do well to cover. To draw such a conclusion was the epitome of naiveté, of course. But I had no one to consult. Bill Nicholas, whom I regarded as a potential friend, was still in Switzerland. So I be-gan to read the magazine in a new way. Critically. And to formu-late ideas as to how it might be improved.

Meanwhile, I was learning about the National Geographic Society as an institution. I was happily sailing back into Victorian times. The halls were marble, the ceilings high. The voices were low, the atmosphere calm. There was a vast gulf between men and women.

For example, the subsidized cafeteria in the basement of the Headquarters building, connected by a corridor to Hubbard Hall, was segregated by sex as well as by position. All the women ate in one large room and were joined by the men only when they brought fe-male guests to lunch. Staff men dined in a smaller room while an even smaller private dining room took care of the top executives. Dr. Gilbert Hovey Grosvenor, editor-in-chief since 1899 and president since 1920, had his own private dining room. Waiters served the private dining rooms, of course, and cleared dishes and trays from the men's dining room. The women bused their own trays.

Not only did women eat apart, but the women's dining room, mostly furnished with tables for seating twelve, was bound by strict, unwritten rules. Newcomers were taken to a table where it was expected they would be happy with other like-thinking women. Although there were some exceptions, businesswomen ate with businesswomen, secretaries with secretaries, and library and research people with library and research people. The Society's lone woman writer, Lonnelle Aikman, lunched with the library and research people, where I had been assigned. No one ever dared change their seating assignment or the time scheduled for the half hour lunch period, and each person sat in the same chair or at least at the same place at the table. Otherwise tempers flared or hurt feelings resulted.

Women with seniority tended to guide or dominate the luncheon conversation. And one learned not to change the topic until a dead silence proclaimed the need for change. I also learned, in time, not to ask too many questions because they often revealed what was regarded as unorthodox thinking. At one luncheon gathering, for example, I asked, "Has anyone ever thought of putting a picture on the cover of the magazine?"

There was a stunned silence and the question hung in the air unanswered until someone introduced a new topic. Shortly thereafter, the question brought me before the court of Miss Strider who called me into her Headquarters office for what can only be called a dressing down.

"I understand," she said, "that you have suggested that *pictures* be used on the cover of the magazine." Her tone was one of incredulity. "You must know, Mrs. Patterson, that it is tradition to have only article titles and authors printed on the cover of the magazine. And tradition here is sacred!"

Warming to her theme of tradition, Miss Strider continued, "And while I'm on the subject, you should know that you have been seen *walking too fast* through the corridors. It is not the custom here for *young ladies* to race around."

Miss Strider's interest in setting me straight on manners crowded out any questions she might have had as to what I was doing to earn my pay, for which I was grateful. It was hard enough keeping the luncheon crowd at bay. But manners were important at the Geographic of that day. No one, male or female, was allowed to smoke in the building. Men were expected to wear coats and ties at all times. Women dressed modestly after an edict came down a few years earlier that so-called "peekaboo" blouses—whatever they were—would not be allowed.

Except for the cleaning and cafeteria people, all the young women hired were college graduates and many were debutantes. None were really expected to work on after they found husbands. But dating single men at the Geographic was frowned upon and one of the reasons for separating the sexes at lunch was to keep married men's minds off pretty young women employees. The other reason was to protect the young women from the jokes and language of the sophisticated, world-traveled men.

The Geographic was, in fact, a very elite gentleman's club, which did not admit women, even though an occasional professional, such as Lon Aikman, was tolerated as a nonmember. That a women might wish to be a writer or editor, as well as a wife and possibly even a mother, was regarded as unladylike, pushy, vulgar, unnatural, and, worst of all, non–Geographic.

I guess I was all the above and more because, within two weeks of arrival, I knew I wanted to make the *Geographic* a lifetime career and someday to be the magazine's editor. Despite all the male chauvinism—and it was not much different from that seen at other institutions of the day—the *Geographic* was a marvelous place to work. The place was small enough at the time for everybody to know everybody—we couldn't have been more than about two hundred, including service people—and there was a real feeling of family.

We all shared in the wonder of discovering the world. Images from the far corners of the earth paraded through the halls. Conversations were filled with place-names from everywhere. Writers and editors, who tended to look down on people who dropped names, took pride in their own ability to drop places. Conversations were filled with the on-assignment experiences of the fortunate gentlemen of the Geographic who would habitually draw a circle of secretaries, researchers, and other staff people to hear of their exploits. But most important of all, the material one worked with daily simply blew the mind. I could tell that by just reading the magazine.

Paintings and photographs of famous men hung on the walls: Gardiner Greene Hubbard, founder and first president of the National Geographic Society; Alexander Graham Bell, second president of the Society; Commander Robert E. Peary, credited with discovering the North Pole; Admiral Robert E. Byrd, first to fly over both North and South Poles; and a galaxy of other explorers of land, sea, and sky.

Through the years I liked to take guests who visited me at the Society on a short tour of Headquarters. I would show them one painting after another and relate what I called "The Romance of the Geographic." Before the painting of Gardiner Greene Hubbard I would explain that he was a wealthy and prominent Boston lawyer who kept a home in Washington, D.C., in the late 1800s. Hubbard and his wife, Gertrude McCurdy Hubbard, had a daughter, Mable, who was deaf from birth. When she was eighteen, the Hubbards sought the best teacher of the deaf to help her. A handsome young Scotsman proved to be just what they were looking for. Alexander Graham Bell, recently arrived in America, had developed a new system of instructing people whose hearing was impaired. The Hubbards hired him to teach Mable.

The teacher and pupil fell in love and were married. When Bell invented the telephone, his father-in-law helped finance its marketing, a fortuitous circumstance that made the Bells wealthy in their own right. In time the couple had two daughters of their own, and when the young women became of age to marry, their parents gave summer house parties on their seaside estate at Baddeck, Nova Scotia.

One summer Dr. Bell asked his good friend, Dr. Edmund Grosvenor, professor of history at Amherst College, if his twin sons, who had just graduated from Amherst, would like to come to Baddeck for the summer. The boys came and, as romance would have it, Gilbert Hovey Grosvenor, one of the twins, and Elsie Mae Bell, one of the daughters, fell in love. As Gilbert had no job and Dr. Bell was getting tired of editing the little scientific journal put out by the National Geographic Society, of which he was then president, Bell asked Gilbert Grosvenor to take over as editor and paid him a salary of $5,000 a year out of his own pocket.

"That was in 1899," I would explain to my visitors as we stood before the portrait of Dr. Gilbert Hovey Grosvenor. "Dr. Grosvenor is the genius who decided that the *National Geographic* magazine should popularize geography by making it easy to understand. He used lots of pictures and human-interest stories that broadened the Society's membership base to take in a wide spectrum of people." He would remain editor for fifty-five years and, in time, both his son and grandson would succeed him as editor and president of the Society—and I would work for them all, as well as two talented interim editors and the brilliant recent editor, Wilbur E. "Bill" Garrett.

But the romance and glamour of the National Geographic Society did not blind me to the fact that I had joined the staff without having been given a job. So I set about to make one for myself. I began writing memos with suggestions for magazine stories to the managing editor himself, Mr. Jessie Hildebrand.

Mr. Hildebrand was a rotund, balding gentleman with courtly manners, especially to women. (Years later, after his death, the delicious rumor circulated that he had owned the finest pornographic library in the city of Washington.) He was a fastidious dresser and a lover of good cigars. Given the Geographic's prohibition against smoking, Mr. Hildebrand daily repaired to a nearby park for his morning smoke.

My very first memo to him proposed that I retrace Robert Louis Stevenson's journey described in his *Travels with a Donkey in the*

Cévennes. After a short wait the memo returned with a little note from Mr. Hildebrand scrawled across the top. "Thank you, Mrs. Patterson. How kind of you to bring this matter to my attention. JH." I was delighted that Mr. Hildebrand thanked me and thought I was kind to have written to him. It confirmed what I had heard about Mr. Hildebrand. He never would say "no" to a woman— but he might not say "yes," either.

Back to the drawing board. As the weeks passed, my memos flew, and the same notes returned. But when I would encounter Mr. Hildebrand in the corridors, he would be so gravely cordial that I was freshly encouraged to try again. Bill Nicholas returned from Switzerland and greeted me like a long-lost friend, saying, "I hear you're doing just great!" He could only have gotten that from Mr. Hildebrand, I concluded, since I was not working for anyone else.

With Christmas near, I felt so happy about my new job that I bought twenty red carnations and gave them, with a Merry Christmas note, to twenty new-found Geographic friends. Mr. Hildebrand was among the remembered ones. But Christmas was also a time of inspiration for me. Why, I asked myself, shouldn't the *Geographic* do a story "In the Footsteps of Jesus Christ," and I set about researching my memo.

Having grown up in Kosciusko's First Presbyterian Church, from my childhood reading of the Bible I knew something about the life of Christ, and the Geographic's library gave me the information I needed about the Holy Land today. The material was rich indeed, and I wrote a long five-page, single-spaced memo, quoting the Bible and detailing just where a writer should go and what a photographer would be likely to find. A masterpiece, I thought. I would take it personally to Mr. Hildebrand and watch his reaction as he read it.

He received me most courteously and begged me to be seated. I explained that I had another story idea for the Geographic and that I hoped to get his immediate reaction, whereupon I handed him the memo and he began to read.

After what seemed ages, he finally put the five pages down on his desk and sighed. Looking directly at me, he asked, "Tell me, Mrs. Patterson, what do you do for this organization?"

Panic-stricken, I began to babble. "Well, Miss Strider sent me to the library ... and ... well ... I thought I was supposed to read the magazine ... and ... well ... and write to you ... ." My voice trailed away in confusion.

Then, very kindly, "What kind of work have you done before, Mrs. Patterson?"

"Well, I was a newspaper reporter in New Orleans," I answered.

"In that case," Mr. Hildebrand said, "don't you think you should write for us, then?"

FINALLY. After three months, I had been given a job at the National Geographic, one I was educated and trained for, one that I wanted above all things. No matter that the job was not on the magazine but in the News Bulletin Service where, like Lon Aikman, I would write geography-oriented feature stories for newspapers and radio stations that requested them. It was enough that I would be writing for the Society, helping to fulfill its commitment to public service by increasing and diffusing geographic knowledge, just as the magazine did.

No matter, too, that it was not the job I had been hired to do, since I wanted no more of *that* uncertainty. Some two years later I learned what job it was that Miss Strider had in mind. Stationed in the library, I was to have been a resource for the magazine's writers, on call to help them research their upcoming assignments. The only hitch:

Carolyn (far left) with members of National Geographic's Editorial Council listen to editor Melville Bell Grosvenor.

No one ever told the writers—or, indeed, anyone else—that I had been hired for that purpose and was available. Just the lucky breaks of the game, I guess, or one of those hundred thousand miracles that happen every day.

The Geographic News Service, where I duly reported for work, regularly sent feature stories to some two thousand newspapers and radio/TV stations. The bulletins generally provided background information on some hot news item, but flights of fancy were occasionally permitted. They ran about two mimeographed pages each, and, what with exhaustive research, painstaking writing, hard-nosed editing, and agonized rewriting, none of us produced more than about two per week. In my newspaper days I might have been required to turn out four or five such stories in a day, but the Geographic News Service operated on another wavelength.

The outbreak of the Korean War provided the News Service with its finest hour. No one in the country knew much about Korea and the News Service undertook to give editors across the nation the kind of details usually missing from the dispatches coming in from the Far East. We researched and wrote stories on the history of Korea, the people of Korea, the customs of Korea, the economy of Korea, the cities of Korea, the terrain of Korea. In newspapers across the country, such information was simply inserted wherever appropriate in the reports of the war. The Society's only credit was the phrase, "… says the National Geographic Society."

One of my assignments was the ports of Korea, a subject that riveted my attention. The China Sea port of Inchon proved the most interesting because it was subjected to extremely high and low tides. Warming to my subject, I suggested that due to the tidal extremes it was unlikely that an American force could invade at Inchon.

A couple of weeks after my bulletin went out, General Douglas MacArthur did, in fact, land American troops at Inchon, creating a second front that helped turn back the enemy. One might have thought that I had placed the National Geographic Society in an awkward position, to say the least, but I preferred to look on the positive side. Probably I had unwittingly been helpful in throwing our enemies off track, lulling them into believing that America did not consider Inchon a suitable invasion port, and thus giving MacArthur the element of surprise so necessary for his success.

I never knew what my superiors thought about the Inchon matter, but shortly thereafter I was reassigned to the *National Geographic* magazine's Legends (or captions) Department.

At last, I had achieved my goal. I had a writing job on the magazine itself. And Legends looked lively indeed.

CHAPTER 4

Adventure in Arriving

For the increase and diffusion of geographic knowledge.
—National Geographic Society Charter

THE LEGENDS DEPARTMENT of the *National Geographic* magazine was under the direction of Mason Sutherland, called Monty, a tall, rawboned Texan and onetime newspaper man. When I met him, he had recently taken over as Legends editor from Melville Bell Grosvenor, who, as the *Geographic*'s first Legends editor, had created the job. Before Melville, legends for the magazine had been more or less tossed in by anyone with a spare sentence or two. The illustrations, too, were picked rather casually, it was said, with Illustrations editor Franklin Fisher spreading out the photographic take on his desk and knocking off onto the floor what he regarded as discards.

Monty believed that the legends should explain to the reader what was in a picture. If clothes were hanging on a line, for instance, the legend should so note. In Monty's view, it was a pattern of emphasizing the *content* of a photograph. He also believed that he could, by himself, write all the legends, and that I and the single other writer on his staff, Jay Johnson, need only bring him the information.

As a writer, I wanted to write what would actually be published in the magazine. Thus began a four-year struggle to learn *exactly* what Sutherland had in mind and to produce *exactly* what he wanted. It was a tough school and he was a tough teacher; time and time again I left his office in tears. But I am forever indebted to Monty for his instruction—albeit impatient—and for his friendship. Under his tutelage, I learned how to make every word count, essential in writing to a space as limited as that given to legends. I also learned that hours are not too long to spend on a single sentence and that perfection is a possible goal, however distant. Not that I or anybody else at the *Geographic* ever attained perfection, a state equally illusive for the rest of humankind, but the yearning for perfection pervaded the magazine and countless hours and dollars were spent in trying to achieve it.

The editor-in-chief during my first years at the Society was Dr. Gilbert Hovey Grosvenor, who resided in a large, wood-paneled office overlooking 16th Street. I never knew whether it was Dr. Grosvenor or his son, Melville, who handed down the edict, but, incredible as it now seems, the verb "to be" was virtually banned in the magazine's legends. It was believed that active verbs created such a sense of liveliness that *only* active verbs were permitted. So all sentences were recast to suggest action, make things jump, leap, rise, linger, stab (as in "the steeple stabs the sky"). I longed for the simplicity and restful ease of an "is" or "were" that would provide a desirable and much-needed contrast to all those active verbs. But style was style and we struggled to conform.

Policy was policy, too, as I was to discover during some stricken moments. I had been given the assignment to write legends for a series of pictures on the life of a group of Asian nomads, and in studying the pictures and researching the tribe it had become clear to me that the people were very poor. In fact, one picture showed individuals in threadbare robes huddled around a campfire and cooking food in old tin cans. To emphasize the contents of the picture, as I had been taught by Monty, I pointed out that these nomads were so poor that they even lacked proper cookware. The legends had cleared Monty, who normally was fine-tuned to magazine policy, and had gone into first proof where they would be reviewed by Editor Grosvenor.

It was then that I got the summons. Dr. Grosvenor wanted to see me in his office. We had never met; employees at my level did not expect to meet Dr. Grosvenor in person. I came to the instant conclusion that I had blown my chances at the *Geographic,* and that Dr. Grosvenor was going to fire me.

As I walked apprehensively into Dr. Grosvenor's office, the gallant Victorian, then in his late seventies, courteously rose and invited me to be seated. I perched nervously on the edge of a chair as he took his seat and picked up a piece of proof on the desk in front of him.

"Now, Mrs. Patterson," he began, "I see that you have written here that these nomads are poor."

"Oh, yes, Dr. Grosvenor," I interrupted with a rush, "and they *are* poor. You can see it by the pictures. They just don't have a thing, not even cooking pots ... ."

"You have written," Dr. Grosvenor continued as though I had not spoken, "that these people are poor." He then lifted his eyes from the paper and peered at me over his pince-nez. His voice rose as he said with great firmness: "We do not call people poor in this magazine. It offends the dignity."

Then, noting the look of distress on my face, Dr. Grosvenor again looked down at the proof and, tapping a pencil on the paper, mused helpfully: "Well now, let's see just what we *can* say."

After a thoughtful second or two, Dr. Grosvenor smiled with the pleasure of one who had found the solution to a problem. Looking up at me, he delivered his answer: "These people use everything they have, even tin cans. *They are thrifty!*"

And so we settled on the thrifty nomads.

The magazine's editorial policy under Dr. Gilbert H. Grosvenor and his successor (for a brief tenure of two years) Dr. John Oliver LaGorce, then *his* successor, Melville Bell Grosvenor, was simple: If you couldn't say something good about a place or people, don't say anything at all. Under that policy, for example, the Soviet Union got scant space in the magazine during the decades after the communists took over in 1917 to the late 1950s when Melville sent professor Thomas T. Hammond of the University of Virginia to do a story on the country.

Having learned policy the hard way and learned, also the hard way, how to write legends precisely as Monty Sutherland wanted them, it may not have seemed too unusual that I was given the chance to serve as acting Legends editor and sit in for Monty when he was out of Headquarters on writing assignments or holidays.

But it was, in fact, extremely unusual. Several other writers outside the department—all men, of course—were tried out as a Monty substitute on legend editing before I was given a chance. That those writers didn't work out was due not to lack of ability but to lack of interest in writing or editing legends. In those days, legends did not command the respect they later garnered. Staff writers considered legends too simplistic (i.e., pointing out what clearly could be seen) and, with all those jumping verbs, artificial.

Moreover, legends had to be written fast. After a set of pictures and an article were approved for publication by the editor, only God or flat-out death could spare the legend writer from his or her assigned duty. Legends had to be written not just occasionally but *every* month for the four to six articles published in a single issue. Legend writers were not highly regarded, either. Witness the fact that they hired a woman—me—to write them. The first-class writers on the magazine were the gentlemen who flew away on months-long assignments in the field and who were given months-long intervals at their typewriters to produce a single article.

But Melville Bell Grosvenor, the first Legends editor, knew the value of legends. He recognized that with the *Geographic*'s superlative photographs as a lure, most readers read the legends first and, ofttimes, read no further. When Melville, essentially a picture man, became editor of the magazine in 1955, he wanted the legends to be so fulsome, to say so much about the pictures, that we joked about the need for rubber type.

Melville was a marvelous editor, with a genius for enthusiasm. No matter what the subject, he would frequently lose himself in wonder and delight over it. Take the matter of spiders, for example. Now I'm not too fond of spiders, but when a set of unusual spider pictures arrived at Headquarters, Melville called me to come up and take a look. By the time he got through showing the spider pictures and admiring each and every one, with special notice to hitherto obscure anatomical details, I too was in love with spiders. Melville's enthusiasm, so perfect and such a treasure for a magazine like *National Geographic,* was contagious.

I remember another occasion when his enthusiasm more or less outran his sense of reality. The Hungarians, under communist rule since World War II, had just revolted against their Russian masters in 1956 when Melville sent *Geographic* photographer Bob Sessions to Vienna to photograph the plight of the Hungarian refugees. When the pictures came back, Melville called several of us in to see them projected. As each picture flashed on the screen, Melville became more and more excited. Finally came a picture that he felt spoke volumes. A Hungarian family—man, wife, and small child—standing on a Vienna street, loaded down with what they had managed to carry with them from their home in Hungary.

"Just look at this picture," cried Melville. "Here is a family carrying everything they own—their clothes, their bedding, their pots and pans, their stocks, their bonds. Everything!"

That Hungarians under the communists did not have portfolios filled with capitalism's stocks and bonds, as did Melville and most people he knew, failed to occur to our editor at that exciting moment.

Melville also let his emotions sweep him away on another occasion that was, perhaps, the most memorable of all for me in the years I spent as an editor at *Geographic.* Monty Sutherland died while I was on assignment covering the Seattle World's Fair in 1962. When I returned, deeply saddened by the loss of my boss and friend, I settled in at his desk as acting Legends editor.

One day shortly thereafter, Melville called me to come up to his spacious office in the beautiful new Headquarters building that he had built, which President Lyndon B. Johnson had dedicated a year earlier. After inviting me to sit down, Melville smiled broadly and proudly announced: "Carolyn, I am making you the Legends editor, with the rank of assistant editor on the magazine. You will be the *first* woman editor."

Then he jumped up from his chair and came around to my side of his desk where, with tears in his eyes and in mine, we embraced. The pivotal part Melville played in that historic moment—the elevation of the first woman to be an editor of the magazine—moved him deeply and, typically, inspired an enthusiastic outburst.

"Now sit down, Carolyn," said Melville, gesturing toward the conversational comfort of his couch. "Now that you are an editor, I'm going to tell you a secret." And the dear man did, recounting an office scandal long known to me and the rest of the staff.

Sometime during our conversation that day or soon after, Melville told me of one reason why he had made me an assistant editor: "You're a fighter, Carolyn, and you'll need to fight to succeed here. But don't bring your fights to me, expecting me to win them for you. You'll have to win them on your own."

As Legends editor, on my own at last, I clearly saw the battleground all laid out. My first job was to get some real writers into Legends. Unlike Monty, I did not want to write all the legends myself. I wanted people whose writing had style and distinction so that the legends wouldn't all sound alike. And I wanted to change the content of the legends. Also unlike Monty, I did not think we needed to point out features one could clearly see in a photograph, such as clothes hanging on a line. Rather, I thought we should explain what was truly important about a photograph and, going beyond, why a photograph had been picked to represent an essential truth about an action, a people, or a culture. I also intended, at some point, to introduce the verb "to be" into the legends of the *National Geographic* magazine.

My first job was to clear the department of everyone except my friend, Jay Johnson, a talented writer, if somewhat discouraged at that point, and to start with a new team of people who wanted to see the legends they wrote published. About this time I became friends with a young colleague, Elizabeth Moize, or Betsy, as she was called, who was chief of the department charged with answering the thousands of letters annually received by the *Geographic* asking for information on a wide variety of subjects.

Betsy wanted to write and she wanted to write legends. After some surreptitious nighttime teaching, I gave Betsy a real assignment, to write legends for pictures taken at Italy's seacoast resort, Portofino. Working at her regular job, she devoted her spare time to the legends—and did them beautifully. Armed with the evidence of her ability, I asked for her to be transferred to the Legends Department. In the years to follow, Betsy became my junior partner in forging a highly motivated, talent-loaded Legends Department that eventually counted ten other writers, a research assistant, and a secretary. As associate Legends editor, Betsy sat in for me in my absences from Headquarters and, upon my "graduation" from the *Geographic* in 1986, she took my place with the rank I had held, senior assistant editor. (Four years later she was promoted to the position of associate editor of the magazine.)

The discovery of Betsy as a legends writer and the method used to find her gave birth to THE TEST. Hitherto, most *Geographic* employees came to the Society through a connection with those already on board. Nepotism, for instance, was considered a virtue since who could work out better than a member of one's own family? Or an old schoolmate, or a fellow church member? Of course, there were exceptions (myself, for instance), but, by and large, having a personal contact at the *Geographic* proved the most useful consideration in getting a job there.

If you didn't know someone personally, other factors such as education and experience came into play, much as it does at personnel offices across America. Being a graduate of an Ivy League school, especially Amherst—Dr. Gilbert H. Grosvenor's alma mater—or Yale, a special favorite, was a big help. Several years of experience working at another magazine was enough to get one a serious interview. Published work was usually considered in gauging talent.

With legend writing, however, such methods of hiring didn't work. As mentioned earlier, no one really wanted to write legends. Moreover, no one had any experience in writing the kind of legends I wanted to see published in the *National Geographic*. Top family connections, fine Ivy League schools, or broad experience on other magazines did not necessarily qualify anyone for legend writing. Betsy did not have a college degree, having graduated from Stephen's, a junior college, and she had no prior experience except in letter writing. But, and this was of overriding importance, she had studied what *Geographic* legends were all about and she wanted to write them. With her innate talent, it was enough. There had to be a way to find others like her. THE TEST became the answer.

THE TEST was like the Portofino package had been for Betsy: a dummy of pictures with legend space marked, the photographer's cutlines attached, and an article in manuscript form. For the test we usually used a dummy and manuscript that had come close to being scheduled but, for some reason, had been put on the back burner. We took care that it was a subject that could be researched in any good public library. In addition, we supplied the job candidate with an essay on "How to Write Legends for the *National Geographic*" as well as four *Geographic* magazines with especially fine legends to study. We gave everyone ample time to do the very best job—a month.

For almost a quarter of a century I gave such a test to hundreds of men and women who wanted to work as writers for the *National Geographic,* since Legends eventually became the entry level for young talent. Furthermore, before reading a candidate's test results, I had all identifying marks on the copy removed and judged the material blind. I did not know if a candidate was male or female; sixteen or sixty years old; black, white, brown, or yellow;

college bred or high school graduate; Jewish, Muslim, born-again or mainline Christian or none of the above; the son of another employee, the daughter of my mother's best friend, or an unknown drifter just in town to look around. Everyone got the same chance. And, most years, out of the pack would leap the talent we were searching for. And we would hire the winner. Through the years, I brought on board the future of the *National Geographic* magazine.

At first, it was slow going. In those days only four, or at most, five stories were scheduled for any one issue, and the top editors at *Geographic* did not believe that we needed more than four or five legend writers who would, of course, sit at their typewriters day in and day out churning out copy. Any late scheduling meant that the writers would be at their typewriters night in and night out as well.

As legend space in the magazine expanded under Melville and picture stories using legends as the only text became more and more frequent, the Legends Department took daily beatings trying to make deadlines and maintain quality. Considering the long lead time between sending magazine text to the printer and the publication date, it challenges credulity that people had to work nights to meet deadlines.

I remember working many all-night sessions, sometimes alone, sometimes with Betsy helping out. On one such occasion I finished an editing job about 6 A.M. and decided to shower before beginning the day. Melville's office suite had an elegant shower, all marble with huge towels, so I headed for it. No sooner had I gotten fully soaped than the water stopped. Consternation! Draping a towel around my dripping body, I crossed the editor's inner office, soaking his Persian rug, and telephoned the building engineers. "Turn on the water, fellas. I haven't finished my shower."

I could only guess at the state of mind at the other end of the phone. But, finally, came a stammered, "Sure, Mrs. Patterson, sure thing."

Back to the shower. The water came on but scalding hot. Back to the phone: "Put some cold water in the system," I begged. Back to the shower. And success. I rinsed off the soap, dried up, and returned to a full day of work.

I tried to relieve the overwork pressure by holding weekly staff meetings whereby I would report everything I knew from other meetings I had with the top editors. We did a lot of tension-easing griping and often indulged in a libation or two. Early on, I inaugurated the Legends Spring Day Out, whereby we all just took a day off together to picnic, play games, go sailing on the nearby Chesapeake Bay—and conduct an informal seminar designed to let off steam. And the Legends Department originated the office Christmas party where everyone came in costume, representing a character out of a *Geographic* picture.

When, after ten dynamic years, Melville Grosvenor stepped down as editor, he was succeeded by associate editor Ted Vosburgh. A careful man, Ted wanted to get his editorship off on the right foot. He wanted to hear from his subordinate editors what state the magazine was in and what problems people were facing. So he sent out a call for a meeting, a week hence. And with that call I found my chance.

I got the Legends staff together and announced that we would count every word published in the magazine in the prior year. With the count we found proof of what I had long suspected: Legends comprised more than one-third of all words published (that fraction was ultimately to rise to nearly one-half). Therefore, legend writers were the most prolific of all the magazine's writers and the Legends editor had more copy to edit than any of the other editors.

Given the fact that most of the magazine's readers read the legends—and sometimes failed to continue on with the articles—the Legends Department gained even more importance. Word-smiths of the magazine, legend writers, I reasoned, should be paid at least equal to the article writers. Whenever possible, they should be given chances to travel as a part of legend research. They should be given an occasional article assignment so that they might have the satisfaction of seeing their names in print. In fact, I was convinced that the Legends staff should be twelve writers strong so that the legend writers could spend half the year writing legends and half the year on other writing and editing assignments—a much-needed, battery-charging break from the deadly, every-month deadline of legends. And, of course, the Legends editor should be paid commensurate with other editors and have an associate Legends editor to spell her from the grind and permit her to travel and write articles for the magazine.

My agenda was truly impressive, I thought, and I prepared to lay it all out at the Vosburgh meeting.

We gathered in his large office—Mr. Vosburgh, some ten male editors and me, his lone female editor, sitting around in a circle. Methodically, Ted called on each editor in turn, asking "What do you think the magazine needs? How are we doing? What should we be doing that we are not doing?" Eight editors before me answered in turn. "Why, we're doing just fine ... couldn't be better ... magazine looks great ... ." Not one word of criticism, nothing but high praise of every aspect of the work.

Then came my turn. I took a deep breath and plunged in. Up to my neck. Each item on my agenda I hammered home. One-third of all words. Best-read copy. More pay. More recognition. More staff. More travel. More bylines. More article assignments. I spoke for 15 minutes.

When at last I finished, a long, chilling silence prevailed. Then Mr. Vosburgh spoke: "Why Carolyn," he said, "we didn't know you were feeling so unloved here."

Smash! It was just the kind of response a woman at the *Geographic* might have expected. Certainly no man's list of grievances would have been so dismissed. I was crushed, but I don't think I showed it. I had learned, by that stage of life at the *Geographic,* that my only way to survive was to be in charge of my own feelings and show only what I chose to show. And usually I succeeded in revealing my hurt or anger *only* when I thought I had something to win by doing so. I found it rather satisfying to see the bewildered look of an adversary whose patronizing manner or insulting words had elicited only a delighted laugh from me, as if I had found him deliciously witty.

I also used my southern background as a cloak, one that allowed me to lapse disarmingly into down-home expressions spoken in a drawling accent. I was the "girl from Mississippi," and I allowed no one to forget it. Respect for me came with my editorial performance but, meanwhile, I used whatever was at hand to quiet male fears.

Perhaps I had, with my southern act, triggered Ted Vosburgh's reaction to my publicly stated agenda because I knew him to be a man who had a healthy regard for female professionals. His own wife, whom he adored, was the editor of a psychiatric journal. He was certainly no male chauvinist.

I remember sharing with him one truly memorable day in the history of Washington. It was the day after Dr. Martin Luther King was assassinated in Memphis, Tennessee. I had gone to a luncheon at the nearby Statler Hotel, given by the Washington Press Club for then California Governor Ronald Reagan and his wife Nancy. While collecting questions for our guests from the audience, I noticed the TV crews packing up their equipment and moving out before the program had even started.

"What's going on?" I inquired of a TV cameraman. "The blacks are rioting over Martin Luther King's death. The city is burning," came the answer. Gamely, Reagan made his speech as his audience melted away in front of his eyes.

The function over, I and the few remaining members of the audience left the Statler to step into chaos on 16th Street. Traffic was bumper-to-bumper and at a complete standstill. People were racing about, overflowing the sidewalks and into the streets. We could hear the wail of police sirens, the clang of fire engine bells.

Hurrying toward the Geographic only a block away, I could see billowing smoke from the direction of 14th Street.

The office was in a state of turmoil. People were anxious to leave and head for the safety of home. At that moment, I got a call from Ted Vosburgh. "Come on up to my office, Carolyn, I am getting ready to clear hyenas," he said. Devoted to his work and conscientious to a fault, the editor, in conference with me, checked every comma, every word, every fact in every legend published by the magazine. He called it "clearing" a story.

"Did you know about the rioting, Ted?" I asked. "The city is on fire."

"Oh yes, I did hear something about that," came the reply. "Are you on your way up here, Carolyn? I want to get hyenas off to the printer this afternoon."

Sitting on his couch, his pencil bobbing over each line, Ted asked the questions about the hyena legends that put his mind at ease. "You're sure about this? Are you sure about that? Do we need this comma? Would you consider a semicolon here?" But not without interruptions.

Ted's secretary knocked and came in. He looked up at her with annoyance. "I told you I didn't wish to be interrupted," he said. "We are clearing hyenas."

"Yes, Mr. Vosburgh, but your wife is on the phone and says it is urgent."

With that Ted quickly rose and went to the phone. Of course I heard only his side of the conversation: "You're quitting work and going home? Well, if you want to, but I do not plan to quit at this hour. I've too much work to do. Carolyn and I are clearing hyenas. The police advised you to close your office? Ridiculous! Well, OK. See you at home tonight."

He returned to the couch and his bobbing pencil, shaking his head in disbelief. Back to hyenas.

Again came a knock on his door, and his secretary, now looking truly distressed, stuck her head in the door. "I hate to interrupt you, Mr. Vosburgh, but the police have ordered the building closed and everyone has been told to leave. The rioters are only two blocks away and burning buildings as they go."

Ted Vosburgh exploded: "I've never heard of anything so foolish. Certainly, go if you wish, but I'm going to stay right here. What about you, Carolyn, are you staying?"

"Yes. Yes. Yes. I'm staying right here too, Ted," I answered breathlessly.

"Good! Now let's tackle these hyenas again."

An hour or so later we were finished: the hyena story, thank God, was cleared. When I left his office I walked up to the tenth and top floor of the *Geographic*'s Headquarters building—with the danger of fire, I was afraid to take the elevator—and looked east toward 14th Street, the corridor that the rioters had swept down, burning as they went. And my heart sank. The sky was black with billowing smoke and streaked with the red of flames. Washington was indeed burning.

The Legends Department was empty of staff; the building was deserted. I gathered up my things and went downstairs and out to the parking lot to my car.

But Ted had been right, as usual. To leave the office was the last thing we should, or indeed, could have done. With every office in the neighborhood ordered closed by police at about the same time, every car of every office worker was on the street or trying to get on the street. The traffic jam was unbelievable. It was impossible to move, even out of the *Geographic* parking lot. The jam didn't break until some 3 hours later. Meanwhile, I went over to the nearby Jefferson Hotel and joined the rest of the staff at the bar.

Even though Ted Vosburgh and I were friends and respected one another for what we were good at, he and other top editors at *Geographic* sometimes had a way of putting things that made me feel outside the loop, as it were. For example, his "*We* didn't know you were feeling so unloved here," as if the magazine belonged only to him and a chosen few. But, as a matter of fact, from the time I arrived at the *Geographic* until the day I left more than thirty-six years later, I thought the magazine belonged to me and all the others who helped to create it. And in every important way, it did.

Office politics aside, the joy of being at *National Geographic* magazine was truly ongoing because of the wondrous materials we worked with daily. No matter what setbacks or slights occurred, either real or imagined, the bottom line was the value of the incredible education that enriched my life beyond measure.

In the years that followed, Ted helped me win every item on my agenda. He was a true friend.

CHAPTER 5

Adventure in History

It is a mistake to look too far ahead.
Only one link in the chain of destiny can be handled at a time.
—Winston Churchill

I F WORLD WAR II WAS THE LIFE-DEFINING DRAMA for most of
the people of my generation, without question Winston
Churchill was the star of that drama. For those of us who had
grown up in the Depression years and had felt the full force of its
ravishment, Franklin Delano Roosevelt was regarded as the
nation's savior. And, of course, for World War II he played a critical part in bringing America into the conflict and fueling the vic-
tory that was to come.

But it was Churchill who alerted the free world to the peril it
faced in Nazi Germany. It was Churchill who stood alone and,
with his magnificent command of the English language, called
out the forces of right to vanquish the legions of wrong. Or, at
least, that was the way it looked to me and most of my generation.
Winston Churchill, his wartime gallantry flying like a flag in the
face of almost certain doom, was my lifelong hero.

And so, when he died in January 1965, I felt a profound sadness, as if a part of my world had died as well. I also felt rushed
because the *National Geographic* had decided almost at the last
minute to cover the Churchill state funeral, and I, to my everlasting satisfaction, was assigned to go to London to cover it and write
legends for the planned picture story.

I learned of my assignment late on the Tuesday before the funeral on Saturday and booked the Thursday evening flight to London. Getting final instructions from the *Geographic*'s Editor Melville Grosvenor, I was given yet another assignment. Mel had decided to cut a phonograph record commemorating Sir Winston's life and death and bind it into the magazine as a special gift for the members of the National Geographic Society. I was put in charge of getting the sounds from the funeral recorded.

Happily I was not expected to do the actual recording myself, having no experience in the field. The *Geographic* had hired an expert, Jack Clink—such an appropriate name for a sound man, I thought—who would fly with me to England.

Jack and I met for the first time in the first-class section of our Pan American jet. For some unknown reason, we were the only two people in the section and I welcomed the quiet, which enabled the two of us to get down to work immediately, talking over all the possible sounds of the funeral that might be useful for the phonograph record. Big Ben booming out the hour. Caissons rolling on sanded pavement. Pigeons fluttering in Trafalgar Square. Military bands playing somber marches. Officers barking orders to parading servicemen. Words and music at the funeral service in St. Paul's Cathedral. The twenty-one-gun salute of cannon. The whistle of the *Havengore,* the small boat that would take Churchill's body up the Thames to the railroad station. And, finally, the lonely wail of the train whistle as the great man left his beloved London for the last time, bound for a country graveyard at Bladon.

Jack was eager to talk sound and it was clear he knew his business. But it was also clear that he was sick. He confessed that he had gotten up from a bad case of flu and overdosed on antibiotics in order to accept the once-in-a-lifetime assignment. I urged him to try to get some sleep and he tottered off to sprawl on empty seats.

We arrived at London's Heathrow Airport the next morning about 8:30, and on the ride into town I could see that Jack, dead white, was still pretty sick.

"I think," I said, trying to sound cheerful, "that you should go straight to bed when we get to the hotel. That should put you in fine shape for tomorrow." The funeral was just 24 hours away and I was trying to ward off an attack of anxiety. Jack agreed.

London was packed with cars and crowds. Already the route of the funeral procession was lined with people, many with sleeping bags since they would spend the night on the street in order to save their prime viewing positions at curbside. Our taxi fairly crept to the Savoy Plaza Hotel, picked for the *Geographic* team because of its location on Picadilly, along the route of the funeral procession.

At the hotel desk I quickly identified myself and was told that my room was ready. I also introduced Jack, who was given the news that his room would not be ready until noon, checkout time. Distressed, I turned to Jack and announced firmly, "You'll come to bed in my room."

"Madam," the desk clerk said sternly, "that sort of thing is not permitted in this hotel."

"But I work with this man!" I protested. And, oddly I thought, my rebuttal failed to change the desk clerk's attitude. (I learned later that the hotel had garnered a rather notorious reputation as a place of assignation during World War II and had been trying to clean up its act ever since.) But no matter. I took Jack up to my room anyway and put him to bed. Thereafter, I went to work.

The first thing I learned was a shocker. The *National Geographic* magazine was not to be given any passes to prime spots for viewing and photographing the funeral procession or the service in St. Paul's Cathedral. The *National Geographic* was regarded, rightly, of course, as the journal of a scientific and educational institution, but such a status in the eyes of the British denied us rights accorded the regular news media. Our important role as the magazine of record for major scientific and cultural events was not considered. The duke of Norfolk, the final arbiter of all matters concerning the funeral, had made the ruling himself. The *Geographic* was not to be given any of the special privileges that would make it possible for us to do the top-notch job we had been sent to do.

And a whole bunch of us had been sent. First and foremost, there was Bob Gilka, the *Geographic*'s director of photography, who was to be the general for our small army: twelve photographers—the best among staff and freelancers—the *Geographic*'s formidable senior writer, Howard LaFay, whose biography of Churchill would run with the funeral coverage; Jack Clink, our sound man; W. E. Roscher, a British gentleman who with his staff represented the *Geographic* in Great Britain; and me.

It was Roscher's job to spread the word abroad that the *Geographic* was in the market for passes that would facilitate coverage of the funeral. We needed passes to photographic towers that had been built at strategic locations, to the rooftops of certain buildings along the line of march, to a close-at-hand view of the steps of St. Paul's Cathedral where the queen and her family and leaders from around the world would stand as Churchill's body departed from the service inside the cathedral. And he spread the word that we would pay money for such passes. For the press of the world, gathered for the funeral and blessed with the duke of Norfolk's passes, it was a chance to get rich or, at least, to get paid for not working. And a number of passes were coming our way.

Lunching with Roscher at his club, I learned that even as we ate, he was in negotiation for a place for me inside St. Paul's Cathedral—for only $5,000, a steal at the price, according to Roscher. He would learn if his offer had been accepted upon returning to his office after lunch. I would get the word whether his efforts had been successful when we all met at the hotel at 5 P.M., a final strategy meeting called by "General" Gilka.

Meanwhile, I set out to walk the streets of London and talk to the throngs of mourners. Churchill's body lay in state at historic Westminster Hall and the line of those come to pay their last respects stretched for blocks. In the rain, through the fog, the human host shuffled slowly through the streets, solemn, silent. The

The body of Sir Winston Churchill moves slowly up the steps of St. Paul's Cathedral, "parish church of the British Empire." Photo by Volkmar Wentzel.

schoolkids in uniform and university men and women bundled in the wool scarves that bespoke their colleges. The middle-aged who had seen all the horrors of buzz bombing, who had fought in the far corners of the world, who had followed where Churchill had led. And the old, many of whom wore the ribbons of campaigns in World War I.

The *Geographic* had only one pass for Westminster and it belonged to the photographers until they were satisfied they had properly recorded on film the scene within the hall. But for the moment, I was content to walk alongside the lines, asking questions and learning firsthand why the people had come. At ninety years of age, Sir Winston Churchill had become the very embodiment of history. And, I learned, many came to be a part of that history. Others came to mourn the passing of their own years as well as the passing of Churchill's.

Too soon it was time to return to the hotel for the momentous meeting with Gilka and the rest of the team. The photographers were already dead tired since for two nights they had been up to witness hours-long rehearsals by the troops assigned to march in the funeral procession. Already they had their shots planned, if the necessary passes for the various locations they had scouted were forthcoming.

And Gilka, who knew just about everyone of importance in the photographic field, had good news. Many passes were in hand, some purchased from other photographers or print journalists, some given to the *Geographic* by friends in the media. But, alas, Roscher's negotiations to secure a seat for me in St. Paul's had fallen through. Moreover, Joe Scherschel, the famous *Life* photographer who had recently come on staff at the *Geographic,* had not been successful in getting a pass to shoot near the cathedral's steps.

In the middle of the meeting, good news arrived. From the Dorchester Hotel, the office of former President Dwight D. Eisenhower called to say that the British Broadcasting Company might be willing to give up one of its positions near St. Paul's steps to the *Geographic.* Eisenhower and Joyce Hall, founding president of Hallmark Cards, were the two private U.S. citizens invited to the funeral as personal guests of the Churchill family. Gilka told Joe to get over to Eisenhower's office immediately to make sure that the BBC would follow through.

Well, I thought, if one place can be gotten near the steps, perhaps two places were possible. So I decided to go over to the Dorchester with Joe and ask the BBC for a place for me. On the way over, I imagined myself in conversation with Eisenhower himself, pouring on whatever charm I could muster so that he would personally intervene with the BBC on my behalf.

But upon arrival at the Dorchester I learned, once again, how hopelessly naive I was. President Eisenhower, of course, was nowhere in sight. His office was in the command of a General Whomever, whose civilian clothes opened the door for a mistake on my part. I called him Colonel Whomever. He called me Mrs. Petersen in retaliation. And he refused to discuss my cause with the BBC.

It was at the end of the working day on that Friday in Washington—and about 11 P.M. in London when the *Geographic* called me at Eisenhower's office to give me yet another assignment: Get the Churchill family's permission for us to use excerpts from Churchill's speeches on our photograph record. I agreed to try. And, of course, I tried with General Whomever. Would he ask President Eisenhower to speak to the Churchill family on our behalf? No, came the reply, followed by the General's only helpful gesture on my behalf. Perhaps I could get Joyce Hall, also at the Dorchester, to speak to the family for us.

Big Ben, in the distant tower, stands silent during the funeral procession of Sir Winston Churchill. Photo by James P. Blair.

It was about midnight when I called Mr. Hall's room on the phone, waking him up. Immediately, he invited me and Joe Scherschel to come to his suite. A man in his late sixties, I guessed, Joyce received us in his dressing gown and ordered a round of drinks from room service. To my request for help with the Churchill speeches, he answered: "I'll call Anthony."

Anthony Montague-Brown had been Churchill's private secretary and the man Joyce Hall had dealt with when he bought a collection of Churchill's paintings for reproduction on his Hallmark cards. It didn't seem to matter to Joyce that we were now in the early hours of the very day of the funeral. He called Anthony at home. And Anthony instantly assured Joyce that he would speak to the Churchill family immediately after the funeral. He added that he was certain the family would cooperate with the National Geographic Society.

Hanging up on Anthony, Joyce turned to me to report success. But I had another favor to ask. "I need a pass to cover the funeral procession and the St. Paul's service ... ."

"I'll call Anthony back," Joyce responded and returned to the phone. But Anthony reported what we already knew: Only the duke of Norfolk could give me a pass. However, would we like to have the duke's home phone number?

I'll never forget the scene. When Joyce hung up he turned to me and, in his midwestern twang, wondered aloud: "Think we should call the duke?" It was 2 A.M. by then. And I answered: "Let's give it a shot." So we called the duke of Norfolk at home but like the smart man he was, he had put an assistant on night phone duty and the answer was no.

We left the Dorchester near dawn, went for a bite to eat and then on to Westminster Hall where, with the *Geographic*'s single pass, I was able to pay my last respects at the bier of Sir Winston Churchill.

Back at the hotel, about 7 A.M. on that fateful Saturday, a British journalist approached me with a pass to the Trafalgar Square tower built for photographers, right at the beginning of the funeral procession. I bought it for a bargain $700. There was only one drawback to that superb viewing stand. Its platform could only be reached by a long ladder. Since, in those days, women wore slacks only for active sporting events—and I had not anticipated participating in any sports on the funeral coverage—I did not have the pants needed for modestly climbing a tall ladder. So I covered the Churchill funeral in black silk pajamas.

The procession was awesome as you can see from our photographic coverage (*National Geographic,* August 1965), and I found my finest writing voice to introduce the event and describe the pictures.

They called it a funeral, but it was also, in truth, a triumph—the spectacle of a nation, a family of nations, not bowed in grief but standing, taller than life, in proud salute to the memory of a man.

They called it a funeral. And kings and queens, princes, prime ministers, and presidents came to pay their respects beneath the dome of a noble cathedral. Yet it was also a soaring celebration in recognition of the heights the human spirit can attain at its finest flowering.

They called it a funeral. But few dramas have ever unfolded with such perfection. Thousands played out their faultless roles on the stage of a great city, and history itself served as narrator. Men marched, their faces a discipline of dignity. Bands played the somber, majestic themes that man has composed to commemorate death. Guns boomed 90 times for his 90 years. Gallant flags bowed. Time itself seemed to stop as Big Ben stood silent.

The rites for Sir Winston Churchill carried no burden of tragedy. If there was sadness, it was for the passing of an age where one man, in himself, could fire the free world to do battle for its own greatness. And if there were tears, they were shed in watching the mists of death cover the mirror of a personality where men had seen themselves ennobled.

The funeral procession for Sir Winston Churchill. Male members of his family walk behind the body; Queen Elizabeth's town coach carries his widow and daughters. Photo by Patrick Thurston.

While all of it was memorable, I was most touched by a sight glimpse from a bridge across the Thames, where I went after leaving the Trafalgar Square tower and watching on TV the service at St. Paul's Cathedral. Churchill's body aboard the *Havengore* was being brought up the Thames from the Tower of London, bound for the railroad station. Along the banks stood the cranes serving London's docks, so grievously hit by Nazi bombs during World War II. As soon as a raid was over, Churchill would visit the area to cheer on the valiant souls who were fighting fires and clearing away the wreckage and to comfort those who had lost loved ones. When the body of Churchill moved upriver, the great dock cranes, one by one, bowed as if in solemn homage to the man whose spirit had given so much strength to so many.

I concluded my coverage with words from Churchill himself:

"If the human race wishes to have a prolonged and indefinite period of material prosperity, they have only got to behave in a peaceful and helpful way towards one another, and science will do for them all that they wish and more than they can dream ... .

"Nothing is final. Change is unceasing and it is likely that mankind has a lot more to learn before it comes to its journey's end ... .

"We might even find ourselves in a few years moving along a smooth causeway of peace and plenty instead of roaming around on the rim of hell ... .

"Thus we may by patience, courage, and in orderly progression reach the shelter of a calmer and kindlier age."

And then, at last, his words of benediction:

"Withhold no sacrifice, grudge no toil, seek no sordid gain, fear no foe. All will be well ... ."

Our work on the funeral done, the *Geographic* team set out to play. Bates Littlehales, one of our finest photographers, then based in London, gave a party for us all, and I brought Joyce Hall, who had asked me to dine with him that night. Joyce had rented a Rolls Royce with a chauffeur in full livery so we rode in style to one of London's best restaurants. After dining, however, I yearned to return to the Littlehales' home to listen to some of the tales of the day's events told by my photographer friends. Alas, when we got to the scene of the party we discovered several of the men—bone tired from days of no sleep—had passed out or were near to doing so.

Another memorable scene: dignified elderly American tycoon, Joyce Hall, and his dignified immaculately uniformed chauffeur loading somewhat tipsy photographers into the Rolls Royce limousine for the trip to the hotel. There, Joyce lined up all the bellboys and, tipping generously, assigned them the task of carrying our fallen companions to their rooms and putting them to bed.

The next day I saw another side of Joyce Hall—the acquisitive side. He called up the duke of Marlborough at Churchill's boyhood home, Blenheim Palace, and the duke invited Joyce and me to tea at the palace that Sunday afternoon. On the way, riding in Joyce's limousine, we stopped at the Old Curiosity Shop, a gift shop, and Joyce tried to buy the entire establishment outright. (It was the beginning of Hallmark Gift Shops.) Thereafter we went to Bladon where we lunched at a pub adorned with the painted works of local artists. Joyce bought them all.

At the Bladon country churchyard Churchill was buried beside his father and mother. Among the flowers covering his grave was a

Leaders of the world with the British royal family gather on the steps of St. Paul's Cathedral to bid farewell to Sir Winston Churchill following his state funeral. Photo by Volkmar Wentzel.

bouquet from the queen with a card in her handwriting, "From the Nation and the Commonwealth in grateful remembrance, Elizabeth R." And another bouquet, "To my darling Winston, Clemmie." A small cluster of violets and snowdrops bore the inscription in childish scrawl, "For our beloved Grandpapa, from his loving grandchildren." All five Soames youngsters signed their names, including Rupert, who at six could only print the letters.

That afternoon at tea the duke of Marlborough graciously showed us the room where Churchill was born and the wall-covering tapestry depicting the Battle of Blenheim, where the first duke of Marlborough earned his title.

All in that memorable day had been possible because Joyce Hall was so delighted to be a part of the *National Geographic* team sent to cover the Churchill funeral. Once again I thanked my lucky stars for giving me *National Geographic* and all the prestige that went with it.

CHAPTER 6

Adventure in
Public Service, Part 1

Presidential Commendation:
In recognition of exceptional service to others, in the finest American tradition.

ALMOST AS LONG AS I CAN REMEMBER, I had my life all planned. I would give my teens to getting an education, my twenties to finding a mate and launching a career, my thirties to having children and climbing the ladder to success, my forties to achieving my career goals, and my fifties to making money. But I always hoped to give the years of my sixties to public service. I wanted to change the world.

I was especially eager to do my bit for world peace. Having come of age during World War II as a newspaper reporter in New Orleans, I had seen what a magnificent effort that city, the state of Louisiana, and indeed, the whole country had put forth in order to win a war. Why, I reasoned, could not such drive, energy, and idealism be harnessed to win a lasting peace? My public service, I resolved, would focus on peace.

In many ways everything turned out just the way I planned. Except for the timing of the years to be given to the public service. My chance to grab the gold ring and do something important for my fellow Americans, my country, even the world, came when I was forty-one years old. And my public service, given as a volunteer, ran for fifteen years concurrent with my work as a writer and editor for *National Geographic*.

I always thought I would write a book about my public service life and call it "A Thousand Lunches Later," because, with a full-time job at the Geographic and a husband and two children at home, the only time I had to promote my public service mission was over the lunch hour or after work when my time was my own. I thought, too, that I would dedicate that book to Charles Reichmuth, the director of food service for the National Geographic Society, since it was he who made it possible for me to offer my guests, at a quality and price I never could have found elsewhere, elegant, gourmet lunches in the Geographic's superb, private dining rooms atop its Washington Headquarters. After a Reichmuth lunch with a generous aperitif of Tio Pepe sherry or a really good bottle of wine, the people I invited to solicit help for my foundation and its projects were wondrously receptive. But I run ahead of my story.

In June 1957, the *National Geographic* published a story called "Through Europe by Trailer Caravan" by Norma Miller, with photography by her husband Ardean R. Miller, III. The Millers and their children joined a Wally Byam caravan, led by Wally Byam himself, to make a most unusual journey for that time: travel through Europe by Airstream trailer. Manufactured by Mr. Byam's own Airstream Company, the trailers were recreational vehicles towed by upscale American automobiles. Shiny, sleek, sheathed in the silver of aluminum, the Airstream was believed the first of its kind and indisputably the top of the line. Revolutionary in design and concept, the trailers were completely self-contained, with toilets, showers, stoves, refrigerators, beds, couches, easy chairs, water purifiers, even air-conditioning. As you can imagine, the vehicles created quite a stir rolling through Europe, never bumper-to-bumper but near enough to one another to make an extraordinary parade.

Coming to a prearranged campsite at night, the caravaners would park their trailers wagon wheel–style, like pioneers crossing the American West, and, with everyone sipping from a glass of something and lounging in camp chairs within the circle, they would hold a meeting. Wally would preside, chiding those guilty of any infractions of his rules of the road, joking over minor mishaps and misunderstandings, and explaining what the next day might bring in the way of sightseeing or ongoing travel.

Of course, the French, first on the caravan's European tour to see this unusual behavior from a group of tourists, would pour into the campsite where they were welcomed with open-handed hospitality and invited to inspect the trailers—the very homes, as it were, of the visitors. Shortly, the American caravaners would be extended an invitation to visit the homes of their French neighbors. From these exchanges, as among neighbor-to-neighbor, Wally became convinced that international trailer caravans did much to promote understanding between peoples—and peace.

I became sold on the idea myself after I flew to Florida, where the Millers lived, to interview them and gather information for the legends to accompany Ardean's pictures. Not surprisingly, Wally Byam read with delight the *Geographic's* story on his first overseas caravan and the next time he came to Washington, he called me up. I invited him to drop by the National Geographic Society to see me.

Wally was, to my mind, a valuable American original, a diamond in the rough, completely himself, bronzed by the sun as befits an outdoorsman, and brimming with enthusiasm and plans. We hit it off famously. Immediately I learned that Wally was planning the greatest caravan of his life: a Cape Town to Cairo saga that he was confident would make history. I loaded him down with Geographic maps and articles on the African countries the caravan would cross.

As it turned out, the Cape Town to Cairo caravan in 1959 was a triumph of the American spirit and ingenuity in the face of almost overwhelming difficulty. In many places there were no roads, and tracks were so battered as to be unusable, forcing the caravan to use railway tracks or barges on various waterways. While southern Ethiopia was, perhaps, the toughest for the travelers, Addis Ababa was another story. They were received by Emperor Haile Selaise himself at his palace, passing through an entrance guarded by two lions. And the emperor returned the visit by calling at the caravan encampment, greeting each family standing at attention before each trailer and conferring with Wally in his trailer.

But, alas, Wally began to show signs that he was seriously ill. Back home, the malady was diagnosed as a brain tumor. Wally was on his deathbed when the idea came to his friends and associates at Airstream that a foundation to promote international understanding through trailer caravaning would be an appropriate memorial to the intrepid adventurer.

I was invited to join the board of trustees of the Wally Byam Foundation, along with such personages as Lowell Thomas, Jr., and Glenn Bekins, the wealthy owner of Bekins Transfer and Storage Company, neither of whom ever attended a meeting of the foundation and ultimately resigned. But other notables on the board took a deep interest in our work and became friends for life: Cyril Bath, president of the United Nations Association; Robert Peterson, King Features Syndicate columnist and author of *Life Begins at Forty;* Brownie Hardison, the Chicago publisher of a trailer trade magazine; and Helen Byam Schwamborn, Wally's first cousin and longtime business associate.

At the Wally Byam Foundation's organizational meeting in Miami in the winter of 1962, I met not only my fellow board members but the four top executives of the Airstream Company: Charles Manchester, Andy Charles, Art Costello, and Jack Garmhausen. The first order of business at the meeting was the election of a chairman of the board. To my surprise, that honor went to me, and I remained chairman for the fifteen-year life of the foundation.

It wasn't, however, as if there was much to be a chairman about. The foundation would be funded, we were told, by a fee of $5 added to each purchase price of an Airstream trailer. The yearly income for the foundation would run no more than about $25,000, small potatoes for a foundation. The yearly interest on such a sum, in fact, could not pay for the annual meeting of the board as required by law. So, from the beginning, and against all advice, I used the principal of our annual stipend in order to do what we had to do. We regularly spent every penny and sometimes borrowed against the next year's income.

Before leaving Miami, I saw an old friend from World War II days, Bill Baggs, editor of the *Miami Daily News,* and told him about the foundation. Ruefully, I mentioned how little money we would have to work with, how limiting our funds would be on any project of importance.

"What you've got, Carolyn," he responded, "is thinking money." And I went back to Washington to think.

The first meeting of the board was called to order in my National Geographic Society office. What could we do with our money that would promote anything, much less something so large in concept as "international understanding"? Don't touch the money for a few years until it built up to a respectable sum? Endow a scholarship named for Wally in a segment of the travel field? Bring a foreign student to the United States to attend the Wally Byam Caravan Club International's annual rally? So the talk went.

But I had come with a different idea, one that had to do with Edward R. Murrow, the famous wartime news broadcaster and later TV star who was then head of the U.S. Information Agency. Mr. Murrow, I had heard, wanted to give foreign service officers assigned to his agency an opportunity to explore the United States when home on leave so as to better understand their own country and thus better represent it when they returned overseas. He was, I was told, actually sending his home-on-leave officers off on cross-country bus trips.

"How would it be," I asked the board, "if the foundation could get the Airstream Company to give us a trailer or two to loan to Mr. Murrow so that his USIA people could travel the country in comfort and take their families along?" Whereupon, the board gave me an enthusiastic go-ahead, the beginning of the incredible support that I was to have throughout the years from those people and two others later added to the board: Dick Pasche, a past president of the Wally Byam Caravan Club International, and Carl Edwards, a University of Michigan professor and consultant to the recreational vehicle and mobile home industry.

Because I had met the important executives of the Airstream Company at Miami, I could simply pick up a phone to talk it over. The answer was yes. Airstream would loan us two new trailers with cars to pull them and would outfit the trailers with sheets, towels, pots, pans, and other supplies so that the foreign service officers and their families could move in with only the clothes they brought from their work base abroad.

The next year, at our foundation board meeting, the beautiful new trailers, completely equipped, stood parked on the Geographic's parking lot, ready for Mr. Murrow's inspection. Diffident, perhaps even shy for a newsman, Mr. Murrow seemed really pleased. In a program we called Rediscover America, the U.S. State Department people would be able to explore the country in absolute comfort, if not luxury. Together Edward Murrow and the Wally Byam Foundation, supported by the Airstream Company, had successfully launched an important program for the good not only of the families in his agency but of the country as a whole, since the more informed our representatives abroad were, the better they might perform in the nation's behalf.

I felt considerable satisfaction in realizing that with my thinking money and the Murrow project, I had identified the long-term mission of the Wally Byam Foundation: to promote through trailer travel the discovery and rediscovery of America so that the world at large and our representatives to that world might see the United States with understanding eyes.

Thus Caravan America was born.

Looking back, I can see that Caravan America was an adventure born for its time. Not only would it promote understanding of the United States, but it could help the nation financially. In the early 1960s, the United States was near the pinnacle of its power but relatively few foreigners were coming to visit us, in part because the value of the American dollar was so high. Indeed, the high cost of the dollar was creating a disturbing trade imbalance, which visitors to the United States could help rectify if they could be persuaded to come here. On the home front, the American tourism industry was just cranking up and thinking along the same lines as I, even to calling itself DATO for Discover America Travel Organizations.

Caravan America. What was it exactly? It was a program to entertain important groups from abroad on cross-country trips by Airstream trailers. To make it work, the foundation needed (1) Airstream trailers—I thought in terms of twenty a summer; (2) automobiles to pull them—another twenty, preferably new and large enough to easily tow the trailers; (3) supplies for family living such as those provided for Mr. Murrow's trailers. We also needed (4) participants from abroad; (5) time—I figured about a month to take each group of twenty families from coast to coast; (6) experienced caravaners to escort our guests across the country; and (7) a lot of goodwill across the United States to help us entertain Caravan America participants. Finally, we needed (8) a foundation staff that would help organize all this.

For Caravan America 1966, I was able to get everything on the list except item 8. As it turned out, I was all the staff we had and it fell my lot to do almost everything. In the final days before the first Caravan America began to roll, Helen Schwamborn flew from the West Coast to put together the tour books—itineraries, campsites, emergency phone numbers, and other vital information that each guest family would need. Helen was also invaluable in a thousand other ways. As secretary of the Wally Byam Caravan Club International, she provided the important link with people knowledgeable in running the club's annual caravans through the United States, Mexico, and Canada. She knew where to go for help. And help came in abundance from the club itself. With Helen as recruiter, club members volunteered to escort the Caravan America parties across the United States, using their own cars and trailers and paying their own expenses. Without their help there would have been no Caravan America. They virtually assured that our treks would be trouble-free; in fact, we never suffered an injury-causing accident during the fifteen years of Rediscover America or Caravan America. Other members of the board, while enthusiastic supporters, were tied up with their own jobs in other cities and not available for the nitty-gritty, day-to-day work of organizing the cross-country expeditions.

The Airstream Company didn't appear to bat an eye when I asked for the loan of twenty-one new trailers (one extra for foundation use since I wanted to send out a press officer with each trip). Charles Manchester, president of the Jackson, Ohio, branch of the company where the trailers would be made, simply said yes. Young, movie-star-handsome, Chuck would be the mainstay of the foundation throughout its life.

At about that time I met James Gavigan, a former Detroit automobile executive who had relocated in Washington and was working as a lobbyist for the auto industry. Huddling together over a drink, Jim volunteered that he was a close friend of the president of Pontiac. "Let's go see him," he suggested.

"Fine. But there's an airline strike on at this very moment," I reminded Jim.

"Rent a plane and I'll fly you up," said my friend, a pilot. And that is what we did. ("Thinking" money can sometimes turn out to be action money.) Pontiac offered the cars and, ultimately, sent along a Pontiac engineer, Barney Wilkins, to accompany the caravans through that first, experimental summer.

Of course I knew that both Airstream and Pontiac hoped for good publicity from their public-spirited generosity. That suited me fine; no one does anything for nothing. But I did make it clear to both Airstream and Pontiac that I was not in the business of selling their products. I was in Caravan America to help the United States sell itself. The goodwill that Caravan America engendered would assuredly rub off on Airstream and Pontiac. That would be their payoff. And they were satisfied.

My letter to Corning brought dishes and kitchen equipment; Fieldcrest came up with gifts of sheets, towels, and blankets. The U.S. National Park Service and the National Forest Service gave us reserved parking in their various facilities along the route. State parks and private campgrounds also offered accommodations free of charge. The goodwill in the United States was most assuredly out there.

Now, about the participants. My idea was that in 1967 we should invite a prestigious delegation from Great Britain to fly to Washington, D.C., and cross the continent by trailer to California, where a similar delegation from France would fly in and bring the Airstreams back across the country. Then, in August, I would send out a caravan made up of diplomatic families stationed in the various Washington embassies—a United Nations on the road, so to speak. The people who participated, however, should be the kind who enjoy camping, who love the outdoors, and who are resourceful and good sports. Where to enlist such people?

Talking things over with Helen and with British and French embassy people in Washington, the suggestion came that we should ask the British Caravan Club and French Camping Club to send delegations. The U.S. State Department could help us invite the diplomatic community in Washington to join in this special way of seeing America.

In the summer of 1963, when all this was ongoing, the Wally Byam Caravan Club International was having its annual rally in Bemidji, Minnesota. I was invited to come out and speak—on my "thinking" money—and tell club members what the foundation was all about and what its plans were. By selling the foundation, I hoped to help Helen recruit the leadership that would guide Caravan America's guests cross-country and arrange hospitality in the communities where the caravans would overnight or stop for sightseeing. On that visit, Helen invited me to live with her in her trailer—my first such experience and the beginning of our lifelong friendship.

I had never seen anything like the rally of the Wally Byam Caravan Club International. Thousands of Airstream trailers filled with Airstream families from across the nation turned up and took their places in orderly rows on a vast field. Dozens of club committees operated at top efficiency. There was a parking committee, a security committee, a headquarters committee, and they even had their own post office. Officers of the club, past and present, had reserved spaces together. Airstreamers with pets were parked in a special section. A huge auditorium was reserved for meetings, and stars of the entertainment world were hired by the Airstream Company to perform. Church services were held with a choir made up of people from across America.

The rally was like a huge house party. The camaraderie between the Airstreamers struck me as exceptional. Most of the club members were retirees and many were people of considerable means. I thought how great it was that people who might have been expected to sit on a porch and rock away declining years were, instead, on the road sightseeing, meeting and entertaining friends, going to special lunches and dinners, and enjoying life to the fullest.

My speech about the foundation, before the largest audience I had ever addressed, went over big. Everyone wanted to help out. Everyone, it appeared, had taken to heart President Kennedy's inaugural address declaration " … ask not what your country can do for you—ask what you can do for your country," and they wanted to do something for their country. Immediately, I saw that we would have no trouble recruiting the caravan masters and others to help our foreign guests make their way across our land.

At the rally in 1966, the president of the Wally Byam Caravan Club International invited representatives of the British Caravan Club and French Camping Club to attend. And in my conferences with them, no one raised a single objection to my complicated plan as to whom should be invited from among their members. Of course I wanted the leaders of the British Caravan Club and the French Camping Club, but I also wanted the members to represent various parts of Britain and France. Moreover, I requested that the guests be of different social strata so that we might have a cross section of society from each country. The latter requirement extended through Caravan America 1970 when the German Automobile Club and the Swiss Noncommissioned Officers Association sent delegations. However, the kind of friction that the cross-section-of-society requirement generated, particularly among our German guests, prompted me to drop it for subsequent Caravan Americas. The experience taught me a lot about national characteristics and class consciousness among Europeans.

A friend with the American Petroleum Institute (API), Ralph Danford, suggested that the API, then in the business of promoting automobile travel in the United States, might give us gas and oil money for our guests. So I called on Frank Ikard, president of API, whose office was actually next door to the National Geographic Society Headquarters. A beautiful man, he immediately agreed to help and pledged $5,000 each for the British, French, and diplomatic caravans.

The logistics of putting everything together boggled the mind. Airstream sent men to drive the cars and trailers from Ohio to Washington where Virginia's Dulles International Airport gave me permission to park them on an unused section of the tarmac. Members of the mid-Atlantic unit of the Wally Byam Caravan Club turned out in force and helped clean and outfit the trailers with the donated Corningware and Fieldcrest products. Bringing their trailers, twenty families—one for each arriving British family—camped out at the nearby Bull Run Regional Park, where the British caravaners would join them shortly. They planned to serve the guests an arrival supper and breakfast the next morning.

A fellow writer and longtime friend, Lucy Post Frisbee, talked an Elizabeth Arden beauty salon into contributing kits of soap, shampoo, and cologne to each trailer. John Meredith, the Washington representative of BOAC (now British Airways), the airline bringing the British to Washington, got into the act and helped us arrange for a room at Dulles to give a party for the foundation's British and American guests.

It was a perfect summer day in June 1966 when the BOAC plane, loaded with members of the British Caravan Club, set down on the runway at Dulles. From the air the British had seen the long line of twenty new Airstream trailers, gleaming in silver, attached to twenty new Pontiacs in assorted colors. From each trailer an American and British flag snapped in the breeze. After clearing customs, the British, led by Frank Collins, president of the British Caravan Club, and his wife Edith, streamed out to the tarmac to hear words of welcome from John Black, director of the U.S. Travel Service, the official tourism office of the U.S. government established by President Kennedy in 1961.

Then the entire party marched down the line of trailers and cars, like generals reviewing the troops, a splendid moment for all. After the assignment of equipment and the stashing of the luggage, British and American caravaners and guests gathered for the welcoming party, drawn by the music of the Tangerine Flake, a rock band organized and led by my teenage son Rick.

Standing on a chair, I spoke to my conviction: "Caravan America is offered as a gift of the United States so that the world might understand our nation better. Caravan America is offered as a gift to you British first because you saved Western civilization from the Nazi evil in the years before the United States entered World War II." Then I offered a toast to the queen. There wasn't a dry eye in the house.

Frank Collins, a genial, unflappable British leader who became a treasured friend, offered a toast to the president of the United States. Later, after a trailer-and-car parade from the White House to the Capitol, my seven-year-old daughter Lansdale waved the American flag as a signal to start the memorable first crossing of the United States by Caravan Americas. The very next day former President Dwight D. Eisenhower welcomed the group to his farm near Gettysburg, Pennsylvania.

Thus we were off to nine years of hosting prestigious foreign nationals on month-long journeys. In time I was able to bring on board as the foundation's executive secretary the invaluable help of Jerriann Cotton Scott, who took over the organization of Caravan America and, on occasion, traveled with the caravans as press officer. In time, too, I would send my husband Pat and our son Rick along as press officers. Although I got to fly for weekend rendezvous with various caravans, I never had a chance to travel with any one of them, prevented by my full-time job with National Geographic.

In that first year, the French came after the British, and a diplomatic caravan followed. In the second year, with the spirit of forgiving our World War II enemies, we invited the German Automobile Club to send a delegation. My requirement that the visitors be composed of varying segments of the society proved almost disastrous since the German professionals had no desire to mix, for example, with the likes of retired policemen and their families. The delegation quarreled on its flight to the United States, and disagreements became so acute that I had to fly to its encampment near New Orleans to resolve the dispute. Standing on a picnic table I spoke: "This is a goodwill tour, and you must start by showing goodwill amongst yourselves." (My speech must have worked because the Germans had such a good time that they passed the word to members of the West German Parliament, who expressed interest in coming too; of course, we invited them and they came.)

I hoped that the Japanese would follow the Germans, and even though I extended the invitation to the Japanese ambassador over a Geographic lunch, the Japanese never understood why Americans wanted to show off their country free of charge. So we had no Japanese visitors until Japanese journalists and their families came in the American bicentennial year 1976. Therefore, we invited the Swiss to come after the Germans, to be followed by another group of Washington-based diplomats.

While all our foreign groups were memorable, the Caravan Americas, composed of diplomats and their families, may have had the most rewarding experiences, because most of them had never met the kind of ordinary Americans who filled campgrounds and visited state and national parks.

I will never forget the Diplomatic Caravan America of 1972. The distinguished Canadian ambassador to the United States, Marcel Cadieux, Madame Cadieux, and their two sons, along with Luxembourg ambassador Jean Wagner and his family were our guest leaders. Urgent business at home kept French Minister Emmanuel de Margerie from joining us but his daring and adventurous wife Helene and their teenage son and daughter came along anyway.

My husband, just retired and thus free to travel, joined the caravan at the start, but I could only wave good-bye. When the group reached Devils Tower National Monument in Wyoming, however, I flew out for a weekend to be with Pat and experience a bit of life on a Caravan America.

It was an awesome evening. Joining the diplomatic caravaners, we pulled out our camp chairs at twilight and sat together in a circle beneath the overwhelming majesty of the granite intrusion known as Devils Tower. Looming 865 feet high, the massive monument made us feel small and insignificant. Its mystery was almost frightening.

Even so, I managed to make a little speech: "You are here because we in America want you to know us better, to understand us more surely, perhaps to care for us, even when we make mistakes. Caravan America is a program that gives you a chance to see us and our land at a grassroots level. Please learn … and enjoy."

The next morning it was pouring rain, and the campground was a sea of mud. I shall never forget the sight of Helene de Margerie, a most elegant French woman, sitting in her car and gingerly driving across the muddy campground—until Caravan America she had had no experience towing a trailer. At one point she became apprehensive that the trailer might not clear the ground. Without hesitation, she slipped from behind the wheel, walked back, dropped on hands and knees, and, almost flat on the muddy ground, peered beneath the trailer. Finally satisfied that she could make it, Helene de Margerie returned to her car and pulled the trailer out. If I had been one of her kids I would have cheered, and perhaps they did.

On another diplomatic caravan, which Helen Schwamborn accompanied as press officer, the counselor from Togo, M. de Madeinos, gathered all the children around before dinner and gave them French lessons. "They were a remarkable family," Helen wrote me, "and even had a sumptuous dinner party one night for all the caravaners, prepared by Madam Madeinos in her Airstream. Their ten-year-old son, Patrise, greeted us in native costume, as did his parents, and served us a special aperitif. It was almost unreal: sitting under the stars in a remote area of South Dakota and sharing a wonderful evening with new friends from another world."

Years later, when Emmanuel de Margerie returned to Washington as French ambassador, his wife Helene told me that her Caravan America trek was one of the most memorable experiences of her life. She said her children were so impressed that they made a scrapbook of the journey. The point, she explained, was that they had seen America in such a unique way, and that she and her children had found such travel to be vastly instructive in revealing the basic kindness and friendliness of the American people. "They yearn for understanding," she said, "as do we all."

For the Wally Byam Foundation's Rediscover America for the U.S. State Department and Caravan America for foreign groups and diplomats, President Richard Nixon awarded me a commendation "in recognition of exceptional service to others, in the finest American tradition." But my career in public service did not end there. By 1973 I had begun my promotion of Open House, USA, a plan to invite the world to the nation's birthday party in 1976.

CHAPTER 7

Adventure in the Stone Age

*One doesn't discover new lands without consenting
to lose sight of the shore for a very long time.*
—Andre Gide

THE PICTURES RIVETED THE ATTENTION. Sharp, memorable images of people, their bodies bare of clothes, stained black with juice from green fruit, their faces aflame with red paint, beads around their necks, feathers on their heads, and the most distinctive touch of all, wooden disks worn in stretched-out slits on their lower lips.

Dr. Jesco von Puttkamer, the Brazilian explorer and photographer, had come to National Geographic with a collection of such pictures, shot over the course of a decade, showing the traditional and changing way of life among the Txukahameis Indians. A Stone Age people, the Txukahameis lived in the depths of a riverine jungle in the vast Brazilian preserve of Xingu National Park.

Of course, we would publish the pictures, but in what form? It was decided to run them as a picture story with long legends. And, because I was the magazine's Legends editor, the job of supplying the words fell on me. But, alas, Jesco's information was scant, not enough to fill the space or properly inform the reader. Someone would have to go to Brazil to get the information, and I was elected.

There was only one hitch. Xingu National Park had been established at the urging of brothers Claudio and Orlando Villas Boas, longtime protectors of Brazil's Stone Age peoples, in the hope that it would shield the Indians from disease and Western influences destructive to their culture. As a result, it had been declared off-limits to white people. But Jesco had gone in under very special permission from Claudio himself. Would Claudio allow me in?

The appeal went out. Word came back: Permission was granted for me to visit the Txukahameis for one day only in the fall of 1974. I would be, I was told, the first white woman in the Xingu.

I had no idea what I was getting into when I set out for Brazil. Of course, I hoped to make a contribution to the *Geographic*'s reflection of Txukahameis life, but I never dreamed that the whole affair would begin with a romance.

It was arranged that I would meet Jesco—who would go with me to the Xingu—in his hometown of Goiania in Brazil's Rondonia Province, where I would stay the night. Thereafter we would charter a plane and fly to the Xingu's Porto Diauarum, where Claudio kept his eye on the northern sector.

Jesco met me at the Goiania Airport and took me to my hotel, where we lunched and discussed the coming assignment.

"Father would like to meet you," Jesco said softly. A huge man in his mid-fifties with a kindly manner, Jesco always spoke in a near whisper. Unmarried, he lived with his father, the Baron von Puttkamer who, according to Jesco, was quite an adventurer. Among other things he had made a fortune mining emeralds in South America, Jesco explained, adding that his father had lost several fortunes, including the one that emeralds had made for him.

"Come for tea," Jesco invited. "I'll pick you up at 3:30 this afternoon. Our home is in the country and it will take a half hour to get there."

Tea at the country home of a baron! I dressed with some care and carried a pair of white gloves. Jesco arrived for me in his open jeep and we went flying through town. At the outskirts our road ran out of pavement, and we hit a track ankle-deep in the finest, softest white dust I had ever seen. Roaring along, the only vehicle abroad, we stirred up an immense white cloud that could be seen for miles around on the flat, treeless plain. Although most of the dust settled behind us, Jesco and I got our share. The blond man got blonder and blonder while I, a brunette, turned gray within seconds. So much for dressing up to meet the baron.

The baron's home was a rambling white-frame structure with wide porches, set beside its own dust road in the middle of the featureless land. There were no neighboring houses or outbuildings in sight. Jumping from the jeep—and creating mini-dustclouds in the process—Jesco and I waded through yet more dust to reach the porch where the baron stood to welcome us. He was a small, slender man, in contrast to Jesco's bulk, with a neatly trimmed gray mustache. I figured him to be between eighty and ninety years of age, but he was quick and lively with fierce eyes that fastened on my face and never left it. He wore a white shirt, which was covered with white dust.

Shortly, out came Elizabeth, a lady somewhere in her seventies, wearing white jodhpurs and a white shirt. Like a veil, dust covered her white hair, face, and clothes. Elizabeth was introduced so vaguely that I suspected she was the baron's mistress. And her manner was vague as well. Wispy, fluttering, Elizabeth spoke in phrases, little gasps of words usually too soft to be deciphered.

But I did hear "tea" and with the kind of gesture one uses to wave good-bye rather than beckon, Elizabeth led the way to a small round tea table on the porch where a silver tea service, covered with dust, had been set out. I was seated to the right of the baron, whose English was such that Jesco had have to serve as translator.

The conversation was largely about me and my work at the Geographic. The baron, flashing smiles, appeared to devour Jesco's explanations in German, while his eyes never left my face. Taking no notice, Elizabeth airily poured tea, muttering little snatches of nothing. I tried to smile at everyone but confusion had struck my heart. Underneath the white, dust-ladened tablecloth, the baron's hand was on my knee.

Wearing my determined-to-keep-it smile, I pushed his hand away and, looking the baron squarely in the eyes, gave a small shake of the head. His hand returned immediately and this time he squeezed my leg before clamping it in a viselike grip. Without taking his eyes off me, the baron spoke to his son in German.

"Father," said Jesco in his whisper, "would like you to know that he admires you very much."

I responded with some inanity, since my mind was whirling with questions: When can we leave? How much more is the baron going to go? What is going to happen next?

What happened next was that Jesco got up, saying, "Father wants you to see some pictures of him as a younger man" and disappeared into the house. Elizabeth, too, rose and fluttered away, just breathing the words, "agua caliente"—hot water. The moment we were alone, the baron leaned toward me, his face in my face and, without relaxing his grip on my leg with his right hand, grabbed my breast with his left hand. "I love you," he said in English.

Thereupon I rose, dislodging both his hands. The rest of the visit was spent with me on my feet, smiling, talking, drinking tea, waving my hands, and moving about, unfettered and untouched. As Jesco and I prepared to leave, the baron momentarily disappeared into the house. Returning to the porch, he lifted my hand and, with a flourish, bent over and kissed it. Still holding my hand after the kiss, he turned it palm side up and placed in it a small leather pouch, closed with a drawstring.

"Father wants you to have this as a gift," said Jesco. The gift was a clutch of uncut emeralds, enough to make a lovely necklace someday.

"No, no," I protested. But it was in vain, as I uncertainly mumbled my thanks and stumbled down the path to take my seat in the jeep, conscious of the baron's piercing eyes following my every step. As we drove away in a cloud of dust, I looked back and waved. Suddenly, I felt a little tug of admiration for those two left on the porch.

There was Elizabeth, blithely waving hello and come in rather than good-bye. In her dreamy, floating way she had learned how to escape pain, and our visit had been no more than a ripple on the calm lake of her life. As for the baron, looking at the bleak finale of an adventure-filled life, lost at the end of a dusty road, he had had a wonderful, romantic afternoon, albeit at my expense. And, if living in the memory of someone else is immortality, he had snatched a piece of that, too, because more than two decades later I remember our encounter as if it were yesterday.

We left early the next morning, for it would take all day to get to our destination in the Xingu. The pilot of our small chartered plane was a young man who only spoke Portuguese, and since I spoke only English, we communicated mostly by sign language and smiles. At noon, we dropped down for a landing on a small strip of concrete adorned with a single fuel pump manned by a lone attendant. After refueling, we strolled over to lunch at a nearby riverside fish house, a cavernous place but nearly deserted with only two other customers beside ourselves.

Back in the air we droned on through the afternoon, flying over what seemed an endless green jungle unbroken by any clearings or dwellings. But finally, a landmark appeared as we followed the broad Xingu River that flows through the park, cutting it in half before joining the mighty Amazon to the north.

"Porto Diauarum is on the Xingu River," explained Jesco. "And so is the Txukahameis village."

At twilight, Jesco pointed down and there below us was the outpost, a few thatched huts strung out on one side of the river and a grassy landing strip then in use as a pasture for goats and chickens. We buzzed the field and the goats scattered. The chickens didn't move until we were skimming the ground and we came to a stop amid flying feathers and loud squawks. As we climbed out of the plane, Claudio Villas Boas walked onto the field to greet us. He was a distinguished-looking man, with a carefully trimmed white mustache and graying hair, of medium build and muscular but thin. He held out his hand and welcomed us in Portuguese. Jesco, again, would have to be my interpreter.

Inside Claudio's dirt-floored hut, Jesco and Claudio fell into a long, animated conversation, leaving me free to look around. The single large room held Claudio's bed, covered with mosquito netting, his desk and chair, and a few stools. Otherwise, it was furnished with case after case of books. Shakespeare, Molière, Hugo, Cervantes, Tolstoy—a roomful of classics, a beachhead of Western civilization in the depths of a jungle where it had been forbidden to enter.

An Indian woman came into the room and Claudio rose and put his arm around her shoulders as he introduced her to Jesco and me, a gesture that indicated she and he were more than just friends. Words in a language I could not recognize were exchanged between Claudio and the woman, whose name sounded like Rose. Claudio then spoke to Jesco in Portuguese.

"Claudio says for you to go with Rose and have something to eat," Jesco said to me.

"Won't you eat too?" I asked.

"Later. I will eat later with Claudio," he answered.

I left the two men about to crack open a bottle of rum and followed Rose out into the darkness. And I mean darkness. Never have I seen so black a night. No lights shown except behind us in Claudio's hut and far ahead in a hut near the river. The sky, too, was dark, the moon and stars covered by clouds. A cold breeze blew off the river and the surrounding jungle was loud with cries. Were they cries of animals or birds or men? I wondered. Uneasy, I began to wonder what I was doing in such a strange place, so far away from everything I knew, so alone in speaking a language no one else but Jesco understood, so isolated in the infinity of a jungle filled with dangers I could only guess at. I shivered with a chill not altogether caused by the night.

When I got to the lighted hut I saw that it was an open-sided kitchen overlooking the river with a wood fire burning on a stone hearth raised to elbow level and set with blackened pots. Spoons and bowls had been laid out on a rough wooden table where stools were drawn up. With sign language, Rose offered me a helping of a mysterious dish from one of her blackened pots. It didn't smell like anything familiar. I had been warned about eating and drinking *anything* unfamiliar

As the first white woman to visit the Txukahameis in the Xingu National Park, Carolyn's sex was a mystery to the Indians—until they felt her body to find out what she had and what she didn't have. Photo by Jesco von Puttkamer.

for fear of dysentery. Thus, I felt it wise to skip dinner and go directly to bed, since our departure for the Txukahameis village was planned for 4 A.M. Sleep would mask my hunger.

But sleep was a problem in the hut that Rose led me to. Small, thatched, dirt-floored, the hut's only furnishing was a hammock strung from one side to the other. I bedded down in the clothes I was wearing, loose denim trousers and an oversize work shirt, and pulled a dirty blanket over me. The remainder of the night was spent in a state of terror as I listened to a lively pack of huge rats scurrying across the floor and speculated as to when they might decide to scramble up the sides of my hut and down the hammock's ropes to meet me face-to-face. The rats were a major deterrent to any plan I might have had to answer nature's call in the nearby bushes, since I wasn't about to risk putting a foot down on the dirt floor.

It was still pitch dark when Jesco called me the next morning. The sound of his voice scattered the rats and allowed me to leave the hammock and hut. We walked together to the riverbank where a small outboard motorboat stood by. Claudio came to see us off and introduce us to a young man, a Txukahameis Indian, who lived there at Porto Diauarum and who would accompany us on our journey. He was called something like John. Our young airplane pilot had been given permission to go along, making us, with Jesco, four in all. Once gathered, we jumped into the boat and chugged off, with John, who had spent most of his life shielded from modern influences, competently steering the boat and tending the motor.

The Xingu is a powerful, curving stream not as mighty as the Mississippi but still a profound refreshment of openness in the dense, impenetrable green of the jungle. As dawn broke, I drank in the peace and beauty of the river, as natural today as eons ago during the centuries of its birth. This was no river dammed by man, with banks corseted by revetments, bereft of its oxbows, denuded of its fallen bankside trees. No, the people who lived along this river accepted it as it was. But that did not mean that they accepted what came down the Xingu, as we shortly learned.

Rounding a bend in the river, I had no sooner spotted a cluster of thatched-roofed huts atop a nearby rise when the huts seemed to burst open, loosing a stream of armed, naked men. With spine-chilling screams, hoots, and howls, they rushed down to the river, pausing only briefly to shoot arrows and throw long spears dipped in poison in our direction. Terrified, I stood up in the boat looking frantically around to see who might be the target of this vicious attack, when I suddenly realized—*it was our boat! Us!* Arrows and spears fell all around us, striking the boat with loud thuds, splashing in the water, kicking up spray. At the same time the band of warriors were wading into the river's shallows, coming toward us.

Suddenly I felt a blow at my back and I was down on my knees, then on my stomach, pushed to the bottom of the boat by John, who firmly planted one of his bare feet between my shoulder blades to hold me down. He gunned the motor and we sped downstream, the attacking Indians still howling, tossing spears, and shooting arrows.

The danger now behind us, I no longer felt John's foot on my back and sat up. "Good God. What is going on?" I cried.

"The Indians are suspicious of all boats. There has been a lot of unrest. Some tribes are at war with other tribes," came Jesco's soft answer, delivered with what I considered monumental calm. "Claudio told me about it last night."

A fine time to tell me, I thought, with apprehension rising. "Are these Indians Txukahameis?" I asked.

"Oh, no. Another tribe. The Txukahameis know we are coming and will welcome us. We can be sure of that," Jesco responded reassuringly, all the while dipping into his knapsack and pulling out handfuls of brightly colored balloons.

"If we blow up these balloons and set them loose on the river, the current will send them down before us," Jesco explained. "When the Indians see the balloons, they will know that we come in peace."

And so we did. When we finally continued our downstream passage and arrived at the Txuk village Porori, we could see that our message had arrived first as the Indians had come out of their huts and the nearby forest to line the riverbank. Laughing and shouting, they waved at us with the balloons they had retrieved from the water. It seemed that we were being welcomed not only as peaceful people but party people as well. And the Indians joined in the spirit. In the warm flood of relief, I marveled at how easily our goodwill was communicated, what simple little things can speak of good times, how eager people are to laugh, to enjoy. Certainly, no balloons at any party I have ever attended did so much to lighten the mood and contribute to merriment than those along the Xingu.

Our arrival at Porori gave the Indians a chance to show us their goodwill: They came out undressed. From Jesco's pictures, taken a few years earlier, I had seen the Txuks portrayed in absolute nudity, save the scantiest of penis shields, but even then many had taken to wearing shorts and T-shirts or dresses. (The title that

Carolyn with the wife and child of a Txukahameis warrior. Photo by Jesco von Puttkamer.

eventually ran with the story, published in February 1975, duly noted the change: "Brazil's Txukahameis—Good-bye to the Stone Age.") But in anticipation of a visit from the National Geographic, everyone had left off what clothes they might own. Some had even had the time to blacken their bodies, get their faces painted in the traditional bright red masks, put on feather headgear and beaded bracelets, and insert the flat wooden lip disks.

Jesco showed his delight at being back among his beloved Indians with a face wreathed in smiles, arms flung out to embrace, hands ready to pat, to squeeze, to soothe. I was forgotten as he made his way from hut to hut, group to group, and person to person.

Jesco may have forgotten me, but I was the immediate center of curious attention from a dozen or so older tribesmen, whom I took to be the leaders. They walked me to the clearing in the center of the village where an open-sided meeting pavilion stood. There, surrounded by the naked throng, I was shyly examined. Their hands touched me here and there, found out what my body had and what it lacked. And the moment of discovery dawned— a woman! My loose trousers and shirt had concealed my sex, and having never seen a white woman before they naturally wondered what I might be—and, just as naturally, investigated. Broad smiles proclaimed their pleasure at the novelty of me.

It was one of the oddest interviews in my long career of eliciting information from people. We sat in the meetinghouse, the naked men and I, and looked at a set of Jesco's select pictures I had brought along. There was a great deal of hooting and laughter, slapping of thighs, and poking of ribs as the men saw themselves, their friends, and their relatives in the pictures. Jesco interrupted this feast of friendship to translate my questions and their answers.

I learned that the lip disks, the face and body paint, the feathers—even the jewelry—all proclaimed the male wearer to be a mighty warrior, different from others, to be feared. They told me of harvest festivals in which men dance to ensure a bountiful crop and other festivals to celebrate the naming of village boys and girls when everyone is treated to baked turtle. I learned about the painful rites that initiate young men into manhood, which include scarifying their legs with fish teeth and holding wasp nests in their hands to demonstrate bravery when the insects sting. They explained how the young men who pass such tests are introduced to sex by highly respected older women.

I learned of the dangers in their lives: the anaconda, a huge snake capable of squeezing children to death; the flesh-eating piranha, a deadly fish that inhabits the Xingu River and sometimes attacks swimmers; and human intruders—the rubber tappers, highway construction workers, even other Indian tribes—the most feared danger of them all. Because they were fearful, the Txuks made others fear them. Until resettlement at Porori, they were considered the scourge of the Amazon basin. In fact, Txukahameis still living outside Xingu National Park were believed so volatile that they might at any moment declare war on their traditional enemies, the Kreen-Akarores.

The day wore on and I spent time watching the Txuk women, who appeared to do all the work of the village, preparing a feast in our honor. They roasted an armadillo with bananas over an open fire. They skinned a small furry animal and boiled the flesh in a pot. They pounded corn and baked a kind of bread on hot stones. They cooked sweet potatoes and squash from tiny gardens they tended in the jungle. About mid-afternoon the feast was ready but, unhappily, I had seen too much of its preparation to be hungry for it. Harboring no such reservations Jesco dined with relish,

Visiting another tribe of Stone Age peoples in Brazil's Xingu National Park, Carolyn is urged to taste a native beer, served in a gourd, and smiles (above) before taking a sip (below). Photo by Jesco von Puttkamer.

having learned to eat the Txuk diet on his earlier visit.

Finally, it was time to go. The return trip to Porto Diauarum would take longer than the one coming down since we would be fighting the current. John helped me into the boat, looking concerned. He had caught me wobbling down the path, a condition I put down to hunger since I had had nothing to eat or drink for some 28 hours. At twilight, an hour upstream from Porori, Jesco asked John to head for shore so that we could visit an Indian village I had not noticed on the trip down.

"These people," Jesco explained, "are also old friends of mine. I heard that they are having a festival to celebrate the corn harvest. We must stop for a moment or they will be offended."

Wearily, I struggled out of the boat and down the path to the village center. Jesco, with renewed energies, was having another of his triumphant parades. The Indians we met looked nearly as unsteady on their feet as I. They looked drunk, in fact. And when I questioned Jesco he confirmed my suspicion. Beer drinking was the chief activity of the festival, which had been going on for about three weeks.

One of Jesco's friends passed him a gourd of beer and he drank with relish. Then a gourd of beer was thrust into my hands, even as I was shaking my head. "Oh," cried Jesco, "but you *must* drink some. The Indians will be very offended if you don't. We can't risk offending them."

I braced for the taste and took a sip. Ugh! "What is this stuff made of?" I asked Jesco.

"Fermented human spit," he whispered.

Back on our boat, night fell and the hours dragged by. It was cold on the river and I was shivering when John took the only covering on board, a rope hammock, and wrapped it around me. Too tired, hungry, and chilled to sleep, I fell to thinking about John, the "primitive" who was born in the Stone Age and who knew nothing about the vaunted amenities of Western civilization.

She is horrified to learn that the beer was made of fermented human spit. Photo by Jesco von Puttkamer.

It was John who acted to protect me during the Indian attack. It was John who kept an eye on me during the long day with his people. And it was John who recognized that I was cold and gave me the only wrap he could find. John, the "savage," had proven to be the civilized one. The gentleman. The gentle man.

It was clear he had heart. It was also clear he was intelligent. What future could he have isolated in the Xingu National Park where modern forces were forbidden to intrude? Yet, how would he fare on the outside with no education and no experience with the technology of the West? He was a part of the fourth world, little remnants of peoples of distinctive cultures scattered across the globe, now doomed to extinction, lost for all time.

The Villas Boas brothers were trying to save Brazil's Indians but they knew that all they could buy them was a bit of time in the hope that they could adjust to the onslaught of radical change. As for John, his quality was recognized by Claudio, who kept him near. Perhaps John had a chance.

It was 2:00 A.M. when we docked at Porto Diauarum, but Claudio was up and so was Rose, busy in the kitchen. The outpost that had seemed so strange, so inhospitable, so frightening during my earlier visit now felt like home. With a warm smile, Rose put a steaming cup of coffee in my hand. She had just finished roasting a chicken and the delicious smell of it almost overcame me. Famished, I sat down and ate everything she served.

I went to bed in my own hammock, in my own hut. And this time, I never even heard the rats.

CHAPTER 8

Adventure in Public Service, Part 2

Certificate of Appreciation:
"... for serving as ambassadors of goodwill, both at home and abroad ... ."
—Creighton Holden,
Assistant Secretary of Commerce for Tourism

OPEN HOUSE, USA, WAS A PLAN to bring the people from around the world to the United States for our bicentennial celebration. The invited guests would stay in our homes, visit our schools and churches, observe our democracy at work, and share in our entertainments. And it would all be done by affinity. For example, U.S. Rotary Clubs would invite members of foreign Rotary Clubs to come; teachers associations would invite foreign teachers associations to send delegations; journalist clubs would entertain foreign journalists, and so forth, throughout the entire range of organizations at home and abroad.

But because no single host or hostess was expected to entertain any particular guest or guests longer than three nights, I added a complication that would require considerable effort to make it work. Every group invited to come would be invited by three different groups—but of the same affinity—representing three different parts of the United States. As an example, the Rotary Club in Bangor, Maine, would arrange with the Rotary Club in Kosciusko, Mississippi, and the Rotary Club in Portland, Oregon, to invite rotarians from the same club in Lyon, France. Thus, the visitors would experience life in New England, the South, and the West. They would be expected to pay their own travel expenses, but perhaps at a reduced rate. And they could, of course, plan to extend their U.S. travels to other places of special interest such as New Orleans, the Grand Canyon, or San Francisco. While the economic boon to the nation would be enormous, the greatest good of Open House, USA, would be in the discovery of our land and its people by visitors from around the globe—and our discovery of them. Now *that,* I thought, would be a real contribution toward peace on earth, the promotion of democracy, and the enhancement, worldwide, of the influence of the United States of America.

But how was I going to sell Open House, USA? I started with the Bicentennial Commission, then headed by Senator John Warner of Virginia. I invited him to lunch at the National Geographic Society to which he graciously accepted. He applauded the Open House, USA, concept and promised to help. How much the commission ever considered doing for Open House, USA, I do not know, because I never heard from it again.

Nevertheless, I had my own plans about what I could do personally to realize the promise of Open House, USA. I was in line to become president of the Society of American Travel Writers in 1975. The organization then was composed of some three hundred actives—travel writers, photographers, and travel editors—and some three hundred associates—public relations people promoting various elements of the travel industry. My plan: to enlist some thirty-five members of the SATW representing various regions of the United States and go around the world inviting journalists to come to the bicentennial as guests of SATW and the Wally Byam Foundation. And for six months of 1976, we would send foreign journalists and their families crisscrossing the country in fifty new Airstreams, fully outfitted by Corning and Fieldcrest, with fifty new cars to tow them.

And—miracle of miracles—my plan worked, largely due to Dave Parker, deputy assistant secretary for tourism in the Department of Commerce. Dave was a member of SATW, and he really believed that our society could make a profound difference in promoting the bicentennial worldwide. It was Dave who enlisted the Civil Aeronautics Board to arrange free transportation for our group on Pan American World Airways. He also brought the U.S. Travel Service and U.S. Information Agency aboard and secured us the blessing of the White House. We were also lucky to have the organizational ability of another member of SATW, Jeanne Westphal, who agreed to coordinate the arrangements in each city and see that we were free to devote our energies to the "Mission." Ralph Danford of the American Petroleum Institution, who had proven so helpful on Caravan America, signed up as Jeanne's deputy for our trip. And Ken Fischer, our newly hired SATW administrative coordinator, was invaluable as our Washington-based contact.

The Mission itself would circle the globe in approximately 18 days and include a program in each participating country of about 3 hours, concluding with a reception, whereby the thirty-five SATW members would work the tables and distribute information about the region of the United States they represented. To assist in that part of the program, the National Geographic Society gave us 100 boxes of Geographic books on American subjects to display and give out as gifts. SATW members, such as Phil Shea, public relations manager for the worldwide Sheraton hotel chain, arranged complimentary overnight accommodations for our group in Paris. The Wally Byam Foundation came up with money for the receptions and luncheons that I hosted in each country for the resident leaders of the press.

I planned to address each of the Mission get-togethers in the language of the country we were visiting. Coming from Mississippi, with speech and hearing impaired by southern slurring, I was no fit student for a foreign language, even despite having studied Spanish at the university level for five years. Fortunately, I had invited SATW members who spoke fluently the various languages of the journalists we would meet, and these members would follow

Carolyn speaks to French journalists on the round-the-world mission of the Society of American Travel Writers, inviting the press to visit the United States during the American bicentennial.

me and explain our Mission to our guests. The fluent-in-languages people would also coach me in making my four-sentence opening speech, which, in English, went like this: "We are you! We in the United States are made up of your people. Come see what *you* did in the New World. Come to the American bicentennial!"

We had a gala send-off at Dulles Airport in September of 1975 with a high school band supplied by Dave Parker. The British Mission was a huge success, with the country's most prominent journalists identified and invited by the U.S. Travel Service and the U.S. Information Agency. Everyone seemed to understand my speech and appreciate its sentiments, and I was even able, in English, to expand the themes of the Mission. The British journalists had heard about my Caravan America program and were anxious to sign up for Open House, USA, traveling the country by Airstream trailers. We even invited several British journalists to come as guests to SATW's 1975 national convention, meeting in the thirteen original colonies. The convention itself, designed to retrace and spotlight our early history, was yet another gift of SATW to the nation on its 200th birthday. And the convention gave us the chance to entertain seventeen foreign travel writers, giving them pre-convention tours in the New England and mid-Atlantic states with visits to Boston, Philadelphia, and Washington, D.C., and post-convention tours in the South.

On the short plane ride from London to Paris, my SATW friend, Bern Keating, who is fluent in French, worked feverishly with me on getting the words and accent right for my little speech. French journalists attended in large numbers, and I was truly nervous when I stood to address them. "Nous somme vous," I began, saying the French for "We are you." But the next words I uttered in French were "And I am naked!" My audience howled with glee. Little did I know. I figured that I was a hit in France.

Rome came next with the Mission planned for the morning to be followed by lunch, a video in Italian, my speech, and a longer talk by SATW's Sando Bologna, who spoke Italian like a native. The only miscue: The day of the Mission was a Friday and, unknown to us, Roman journalists take Friday off and head for the country. When the houselights went off for the video that preceded my speech, the journalists slipped out of the hall and I spoke my faulty Italian to rows of empty seats.

From the beginning, I dreaded the Greek Mission most, largely because the Greek alphabet did not easily lend itself to translation into Mississippi sounds. Constantine Savalas, the brother of TV star Telly Savalas, was, at that time, representing the U.S. Information Agency in Athens and had been put in charge of our Mission to Greece. Connie undertook to help me with my speech. We would stroll the streets of the capital, practicing, practicing, practicing.

Finally, Connie said dubiously, "Let's go to my office, Carolyn, and you can make your speech to my Greek secretary. If she thinks you are doing the language well enough, it's a go." In Connie's office, after greeting his secretary, I took a deep breath and repeated my four sentences in what I thought was Greek. At the conclusion, the secretary burst into tears.

"We can't let her make this speech," she cried. "Giscard de Stang, the French premier, was here last week and spoke flawless Greek. The journalists will make the comparison and American prestige will be badly hurt!" Now that hurt my feelings and I determined to continue practicing.

Our Mission was at the King George Hotel in downtown Athens, arranged by SATW member Connie Soloyanis, directly across the square from the government palace. We received our guests in the morning before lunch and the U.S. ambassador himself came to introduce me. If I had been nervous in France, I was more than terrified in Greece. When I stood before our Greek guests, I gripped the podium so hard that my hands ached for hours thereafter. I attacked the Greek words with such earnestness and force that I was truly awesome, I was told later. Whether I actually uttered a single word in the Greek language will never be known, but my *desire* to speak Greek so impressed my listeners that as I concluded they were on their feet, roaring approval. They even tossed the flowers on the tables at my feet. Someone shouted: "She's better than Giscard de Stang!" Of course I wasn't but I did learn a valuable lesson. All you have to do is show people you really care and the rest doesn't matter. I had shown our Greek guests that my heart yearned to speak their language, and it was enough.

The German Mission, near Frankfurt, was planned for the late afternoon and I was to speak after the reception. But most of the German journalists enjoyed themselves so much over the drinks that they accorded my speech, if they heard it at all, with thunderous applause.

And then we were off to Bangkok, Hong Kong, and Tokyo, where I did not attempt the languages spoken there. The prime minister of Japan received me for a private audience, arranged by Bob Fisher, the member of our SATW Mission who was fluent in Japanese. A Fodor travel guide editor, formerly stationed in Japan, Bob was a longtime friend of the Japanese official who helped us recruit the journalists for a crossing of the United States in those fifty Airstreams the following year.

We arrived home some 19 days and 6 hours after leaving U.S. shores, having met 357 journalists during 100 hours of press briefings, with each member of our group giving about 10 hours for one-on-one meetings. Someone counted that we had spent 57 hours in flight, 40 hours in the group's transportation, and 20 hours at airports. Needless to say we were marvelously assisted by the support of USTS's overseas directors: Beverly Miller in London, Paul Guidry in Paris, Hans Regh in Frankfurt, and Fritz Schmitz in Tokyo.

And we came back singing "Glory, Glory Bicentennial!" to the familiar tune of "Glory, Glory Hallelujah!" It went like this:

We have carried high the message
first to rainy London town.
Then to Paris, Rome, and Athens
with a smile and scarce a frown.

Then came Mainz before the long hop,
when in Bangkok we came down,
As we went flying on.

Glory, Glory Bicentennial
Glory, Glory Bicentennial
Glory, Glory Bicentennial
As we went flying on!

After Thailand came a two-day stop
in scenic old Hong Kong
Then to Tokyo for finale,
so exhausted but still strong.

Nineteen days after departure
we still wing our way along.
Did we go flying on!

The least I can do for that valiant band from the Society of American Travel Writers is to record their names in this book that recalls their exploits. The late Betty Blake of the Delta Queen Steamship Line was our press officer. The others, including those previously mentioned, were: Ginny Ade, Len Barnes, David Hunter, Franke Keating, Sylvia McNair, Connie Sherley, the late Windsor P. Booth, the late John Bowen, Betty Ross, Inga Rundvold (Hook) Kuhn, the late Ben Carruthers, William Davis, Landt and Lisl Dennis, Barbara L. Gillam, Eunice Telfer Junkett, Rosamond Massow, Ralph H. Peck, Dale Remington, the late Florence Somers, Florence Lemkowitz, Jim Woodman, Toni Chapman, Michele and Thomas M. Grimm, Yoram Kahana, Bill Simar, and Bob and Norma Spring. Our round-the-world trip and the convention that followed were hailed as "SATW's Finest Hour."

For the bicentennial year Open House, USA, entertained 300 journalists with their families on month-long countrywide tours and won a Certificate of Appreciation from the U.S. Department of Commerce, which reads: "Presented to the Society of American Travel Writers for serving as ambassadors of goodwill, both at home and abroad, and contributing to the success of Caravan America during the Nation's Bicentennial—1976." Signed: Creighton Holden, Assistant Secretary of Commerce for Tourism.

I have never given up having an Open House, USA, on a continuing basis with all of America taking part, as I originally dreamed it. So I urge President William Jefferson Clinton to proclaim the year 2000 as the first Open House, USA, year of the new millennium, to get the nation to invite the world, and to leave office having given a great gift to world understanding and peace.

CHAPTER 9

Adventure in Haiti

We act as though comfort and luxury were the chief requirements of life,
when all we need to make us happy is something to be enthusiastic about.
—Charles Kingsley

Dawn comes almost unnoticed in a Haitian day that has no real
beginning, no definite end. It is my first night in the thatch-
roofed, one-room cottage I have built for a sojourn in Labadi, a
north-coast village. And sleep has not come.

I have listened through the night to the cries of children,
oddly still at play on the beach at my door. I have heard fisher-
men dragging their homemade boats up onto the wet sand or
down to the water—the hour makes no difference whether they
come or go.

Even so, my ear failed to tell me when the gifts arrived.

With the coming of light, I open my door and look out.
Women are up and about, preparing for an hours-long walk to
market in Cap Haïtien. Farmers heading for mountainside
gardens call out to one another in Creole, a native brew of
language beyond my understanding.

That's when I discover the gifts: four freshly husked coconuts, a
tremendous conch shell with fluted mouth of gold, a large crab.

I have come to live among a people so beset with poverty
that an income equivalent to $100 a year is a bonanza. I am
white in an all-black village. I am a stranger who can communi-
cate only with frowns or smiles. Yet I am welcomed with gifts.

A party of men approaches. They stop at my terrace and
display another present, this time of a remarkable sight. In their
arms is a 4-foot-long snake, a native boa, now dead.

It is a prize, and the men watch my face to glimpse my astonishment, my delight. I cry sounds of wonder, and they smile broadly at me, at one another. Then, proudly, they withdraw. The snake, I am thankful to see, goes with them.

WITH THESE WORDS I BEGAN MY STORY on Haiti for the *National Geographic* magazine. Published in January 1976, it was called "Haiti: Beyond Mountains, More Mountains" after an old Creole saying that describes both the land and the life of the black republic in the Caribbean. Haiti: second independent nation in the Western Hemisphere, after the United States of America; born of the world's only successful insurrection of slaves; tragically misruled throughout its existence and now so poor that it ranks among the three most impoverished nations on earth.

During my coverage in the mid-1970s, Haiti was virtually without roads to connect its major towns, and the roads that did exist were so rutted and pocked that it was a nerve-jerking, bone-jarring experience to ride along them, even at a slow speed. I remember traveling from the capital of Port-au-Prince to the southern port town of Jacmel, a distance of 50 miles. It took all day and required a four-wheel-drive jeep to navigate a route that used a shallow river as a roadbed for much of the way. A century earlier, it was said to have been easier to go from Jacmel to France by ship than from Jacmel to Port-au-Prince overland. It was still the case.

Another problem in Haiti was a telephone service so erratic as "to provoke a sense of thanksgiving with every successful connection," as I wrote. To make appointments or organize excursions, I learned to send written messages by hand and hope for some kind of answer to be returned by the same messenger. With such hit-or-miss methods, my coverage of the country developed in a kind of slow motion with unexpected dead ends, unexplained detours, and unsolved mysteries.

For the coverage of Port-au-Prince I lived in the Villa Creole, a bright, airy hotel on a mountain top near Pétionville, a suburb of the capital. The hotel was the property of Dr. Assad, a former cancer specialist who went broke treating patients unable to pay. A man of grave charm, he first alerted me to my "tail," a man sent to the hotel by the Haitian government, then headed by president-for-life "Baby Doc" Jean-Claude Duvalier, to keep track of my activities and follow me around. The tail and I saw so much of each other that we fell to speaking, bidding one another good morning and good evening. It was rather reassuring, in a way, to spot his familiar figure lurking about, trying to look invisible, during my visits to the city's public buildings and monuments. But I had to elude him when I had appointments to talk privately with individual Haitians. One informant told me that "Papa Doc" Duvalier, the dictator who preceded his son, "made fear a pervading part of Haitian life." And that fear still pervaded.

From my privileged position in a luxury hotel built for tourists, I could catch only an occasional glimpse of the real life of the Haitian people. And I wrote of two such glimpses that remain bright in memory:

With friends I am returning from a Sunday drive in the country near Port-au-Prince, the capital. It is just before Mardi Gras; the road is alive with people on foot, in overflowing rattletrap buses, in tap-taps—rainbow-colored pickup trucks fitted out for passengers and bearing such names as "Grandeur of Jesus," "God Before All," "Mother of Christ."

We round a curve and come upon a throng that slows all traffic to the pace of a dance, a dance fired by a five-piece orchestra on a creeping truck. And, in all the flashing color, the wild music under the whip of drum, the ceaseless gyrations of bodies, I nearly miss seeing her.

She stands beyond the roadside ditch behind a wire fence that she is using for a clothesline. She is young and slim and beautiful.

She sees the truck and the people; she hears the music. She is transformed. One hand drops the wet clothes and flies with the other high over her head. Her body, all vivid life and grace, begins to swing with the rhythm of the music. It is no less than an instant of purest pleasure—for her in the doing, for me in the watching.

Again, another time, another place:

As others, I am caught up in Carnival, that last moment of abandon before Ash Wednesday and the penance of Lent. My station, on the bed of a truck, is along the route of a parade through Port-au-Prince that is splashed with tinsel glitter, gaudy color, and music amplified to an assault on the ear.

At the beginning the truck is the resort of middle-aged adults, some seated comfortably on folding chairs. Soon, however, a slow but steady tide of children rises, first to the truck bed, then to its cab. I stand amid them, feeling not unlike a post, available to provide a steadying touch when, in the excitement, someone nearly topples from his perch.

A friend tosses me a package of candy mints. I peel one off for myself and detach another for my nearest young neighbor, whose mouth is only a couple of inches from mine.

"Merci," he whispers, wide-eyed and solemn. Turning, he breaks the small candy in two and passes a piece to a friend, whose own "merci" comes to me like an echo.

I peel off another candy ring for the little face beside me. This time the two pieces go to other kids.

"Merci … merci."

With one roll of mints and another one and still one more, I feed the multitude and listen to the "thank you's" from all over the truck.

No one has more than a taste. But the sweetness of that exchange on a street in Port-au-Prince is truly abundant.

Such brief glimpses only whetted my appetite for experiences with the Haitian people more personal, more meaningful than afforded me by living in a hotel. I would go to live in a village, I resolved, where Haitian life remains largely unadulterated by outside influences.

Because the roads were poor to nonexistent, I thought at first that I should organize a horseback-riding expedition into the countryside. And, with that in mind, I asked my office to buy for me a portable potty to take along. (On that trip to Jacmel I had discovered that privacy for nature's needs was impossible since there were no gas stations with toilet facilities and no bush could conceal one from the eyes of an ever-present throng of passersby and farmers.)

I also requested a pair of walkie-talkies, which I envisioned might be necessary to signal for help should an emergency develop during a trek across Haiti. The equipment duly arrived as a part of the luggage of a Miami friend, Edith Newman, who as the wife of Stuart Newman, the public relations counsel for Haiti's Tourism Department, was spared the usual inspection by customs officers.

The night of Edith's arrival at the Villa Creole, we decided to test out the walkie-talkie equipment. With Edith in her room and me in mine, we fiddled with the switches and began to exchange a few stilted, self-conscious pleasantries to test the machines. Then we heard the sirens. Beyond the hotel's walls the army had arrived on the double, and with searchlights sweeping the streets, soldiers dashed hither and yon, looking for the spies who were communicating in an English code over illegal walkie-talkies. Saved by the bell, as it were, Edith and I discontinued our test and retired the equipment to the bottom of a suitcase. Edith sneaked them out of the country when she returned to Miami after our visit together to the Citadel, the massive mountaintop fortress near Cap Haïtien that was built in the early 1800s by Haiti's first king, Henry Christophe.

It was on that trip to the Citadel that I saw a Haitian home under construction and got the idea that I might build a house of my

On assignment in Haiti, Carolyn has a native-style hut constructed for her use in the seaside village of Labadie. Photo by Thomas Nebbia.

own in a village rather than attempt to camp out on a horseback-riding expedition. Moreover, riding horses up the steep trail to the Citadel gave me all I ever wanted of that mode of transportation in that country. The people are too poor themselves to properly care for their animals, and it was heartbreaking to see the bony, thin, undernourished horses stumbling up the rocky path, their eyes glazed with suffering.

Also, the army was suspicious of me on the move. When Edith and I decided to spend the night at the unoccupied Citadel, along with the talented and charming *National Geographic* photographer Tom Nebbia and my niece, Patricia Bennett, the army dispatched a soldier to check up on us. He arrived just as darkness fell to find us encamped in the so-called king's billiard room, where we had built a fire and were waltzing to music on my tape recorder. The poor fellow was exhausted and, after sharing our food and wine, fell instantly to sleep. We wrapped a blanket around him and let him be, hoping that he would have enough of a report to satisfy his superiors the next day.

But where should I build my house and who should I get to build it? Enter Walter Bussinius, the owner-manager of the Mt. Jolie Hotel in Cap Haïtien, the capital of the colony when France ruled the land and now the chief city of the north. Walter, who inherited his blond good looks from his German father and his concern over the plight of the Haitian people from his Haitian mother, had proven a good friend and teacher during my stops in his hotel. He knew of a seaside village, called Labadi, whose head man, Gerard Almajor, was a person to be trusted and who might be willing to help me. Walter volunteered to take me to Labadi to investigate the situation. So we set out in his four-wheel-drive jeep.

The road—if one could call it that—was a grueling obstacle course of potholes, rocks, eroded slopes, steep inclines, and precipitous dips. We had only 5 miles to go from Cap Haïtien to the spot where the road stopped on the side of a mountain, but it took us 2 hours to make it. Throughout the journey Walter would stop the jeep to talk earnestly in Creole with ragged men and women on foot, who poured out their troubles to him. After such encounters Walter's face sagged with anxiety. So many counted on him for help. Too many for one man to handle.

At the road's dead end, Walter explained that Labadi could be reached only by boat or on foot. He pointed across a beautiful cove to a cluster of thatch-roofed houses set amidst towering trees at the foot of a mountain. "That's Labadi," he said. "The people there have already spotted my jeep and will soon send a boat to fetch us." He led the way to a trail down the mountain to the beach.

The whole village came out to meet us when, after crossing the cove, we splashed ashore at Labadi. Walter's speech in Creole met with smiling approval. "This lady," he explained about me, "comes from the United States and she wants to live here with you. She wants you to build her a house like one of your houses and she will pay you for your labor. After she lives here for a while, she will give the house to your village of Labadi so that you can rent it to make money for the benefit of all. She will name her house Habitation Amitié, the House of Friendship, because she wants you to know that she comes to you in friendship."

Gerard Almajor led the way to the site where my house

The Labadie hut from the back. An open-air dining porch at center separates the kitchen (right) from the bath (left), which contains the only flush toilet in the village. Photo by Thomas Nebbia.

would be built. I was never able to discover who actually owned the land, but since I planned to be only a temporary occupant, it didn't matter. As Almajor lived nearby, I concluded the land must be his. The house site was away from the village itself, about a 20-minute walk, and faced a secluded beach alongside the cove, which was protected from sharks by a coral reef. Across the cove from the beach was another strand separating the waters of the cove from the Atlantic Ocean where long, white breakers rolled in on yet another shoreline of white sand. As a lover of beaches and the sea, I found the situation perfection itself.

Almajor and I discussed, with Walter as translator, the floor plan of my house. Haitian houses that I had seen were chopped up into tiny rooms, to afford as much privacy as possible to the members of usually large families. I wanted one large room with wide built-in benches, fitted with foam rubber mattresses for sofa beds, and a large table for writing. French doors—wooden, of course—should open out onto a terrace facing the sea. Behind the large room, I planned for a kitchenette on one side and a dressing room on the other, separated by a small covered porch for dining.

The walls would be of woven sticks, plastered with sand and mud. The roof would be thatched, like all the others in the village. I wanted a concrete floor. And I wanted a toilet, a regular flush toilet with running water for my dressing room. Was it possible?

Walter and Almajor consulted. There was no running water in the village, except that of the polluted brook that flowed through it. To bring home a bucket of water, my neighbors had to walk to the stream—40 minutes round-trip. Then Walter recalled an abandoned well, high on the mountain behind my house. The French had dug the well in the 1700s and it had not been used since they departed, it was thought. Could Almajor have the well cleaned out? Would I be willing to buy a battery-operated pump? Could I have some plastic piping sent from Miami? Yes. Yes. Yes.

In time, Stuart Newman, marvelously supportive throughout my coverage, shipped us the plastic piping and we installed not only a toilet but a shower bath and a water spigot in the yard so that my neighbors would have clean water and be spared the arduous trek to the village stream.

Getting the toilet to Labadi was a saga in itself. Walter donated the furnishing, one retired from his hotel during a renovation, and Almajor came for it in his outboard motor dingy, traveling across open ocean from Labadi to Cap Haïtien. My husband, Pat, down from Washington for a visit, and I volunteered to accompany Almajor back to Labadi to help keep the toilet in the boat as it churned through the ocean swells. The trip was so rocky that Pat, eventually, had to sit on the toilet to keep it from rolling around in the small boat and, perhaps, tipping it over. I will never forget the

A cow arrives at the front door of Carolyn's hut to give milk for her kitten. Photo by Thomas Nebbia.

sight of my husband, a picture of bearded dignity, grandly enthroned on the toilet as we rolled and tossed on the hours-long trip to Labadi.

When I started living in my completed house, the toilet became famous throughout the region. Since it was the first one installed there, people walked in from miles around hoping to see it and watch it flush. Little groups suddenly appeared at my terrace, smiled, and waited. I quickly learned that they were sightseers and waved them inside where I displayed my treasure and showed its flushing talents. There were lots of giggles of delight and murmurs that I knew to be expressions of thanks for my courtesy.

During the building of the house, I came often to check on the progress of construction. But I was not the only one, as Walter reported to me. Ever suspicious as to what I was up to, the government sent some people to Labadi to question the villagers. At a meeting in the open-sided shed that served as a school, the government men ordered the villagers to have no part of me and my house. "But," said Almajor, "you in the government do nothing for us here at Labadi. Madam Patterson gives us money to build the house and will give us the house to rent after she is gone. We intend to help her." It took courage to face down threats from those in authority; Almajor was certainly a man to be trusted.

The house at Labadi cost $500 and was furnished with homemade Haitian furniture for $500. I figured I saved the National Geographic Society at least $1,000 by living in the house rather than in one of Haiti's luxury hotels.

And, naturally, I gave a party to celebrate the completion of the house and the start of my sojourn in it. Although I didn't actually invite anyone from Port-au-Prince, the government decided to take part in the celebration anyway and sent a planeload of officials. I invited Walter and his family, several Cap Haïtien friends, and several nuns and priests from Cap Haïtien who often came to Labadi to minister to the people. And, of course, I invited all the villagers in Labadi, about eight hundred.

It was truly a gala occasion. Everyone, it appeared, had at least one nice thing to wear. Men, woman, and children who habitually wore rags turned up in hole-free trousers and clean, freshly starched, and meticulously ironed shirts and dresses. A tall, grave priest, Father André Lebarzic, joined a bevy of little girls in pastel dresses and hair bows to dance a rollicking ring-around-the-rosy. With money supplied from my Geographic expense account, the women of Labadi concocted a feast of goat stew and vegetables with rice and brought out a fiery homemade rum to drink. A group of young men with beat-up guitars and a drum sang a song they had composed: "God sent you to us, Lady Patterson" went the refrain. Then they played the merengue and everyone danced on the beach.

I dedicated Habitation Amitié "as an expression of friendship between the people of the United States and Haiti."

Almajor responded: "Thank you for coming here to our home from your great and remote country we know only by name. When you landed, you said how beautiful you found the village and for this reason, how could we not love it more, we who live here? Sometimes we ask ourselves what are you coming to see here? Is it the spring? Is it the beaches and the mountains?

"We think the answer is this: You are in search of one place where the beauty of creation is still bursting!"

And so I began my life at Labadi. A kitten came to live with me and I named him Jollicouer, after a shadowy man-about-Port-au-Prince whom I had met and who was reputed to be the model for the government agent in Graham Greene's novel about Haiti, *The Comedians*. And for the feline Jollicouer I had the village cow stop by my terrace every morning to give us a cup of milk for 5 cents. I felt indebted to the kitten because he kept my thatch roof free of mice—or at least free of the sight of them. But not free of huge, hand-sized spiders.

Every night the spiders crawled down from the thatch to hang mid-way along the whitewashed wall. Their bright eyes shining in the pitch black, the spiders struck me as shy but curious. I hoped that they would keep their distance, even though I knew from *National Geographic* articles that spiders are regarded as friends of humans. Jollicouer, at the foot of my bed, would sleep through those night-long inspections, a reassuring fact in itself.

I spent my days visiting with the villagers, shopping for food—fresh langouste from nearby waters, chickens, and vegetables right out of

Coral protects the cove in front of Carolyn's hut from sharks. The open sea lies beyond the island in the distance. Photo by Thomas Nebbia.

the garden—and swimming and snorkeling among the exquisite tropical fish that lived in the coral-strewn waters at my front door.

And I entertained. Edith came once more from Miami to visit me. A registered nurse, she brought a small store of medicines and set up shop on my terrace, ministering to the cuts and scrapes of the small fry. Afterward we would sit, looking out at the sea, and daydream. I would become ambassador to Haiti and establish guest houses all across the land so that many visitors might have the experience with the Haitian people that I was enjoying—and leave behind sorely needed money for the host village. Each guest house would have space for a clinic where Edith would teach nurses aides to operate a dispensary for the sick.

And, of course, my brilliant *Geographic* photographer, Tom Nebbia, made regular visits to record the life of the village and my experiences among my all-black neighbors. Tom had the enthusiasm and energy of a child with the talent of a sophisticated adult— a wondrous combination. On one occasion he brought Gitte, the lovely Danish girl who became Mrs. Nebbia. And we would sit on my terrace, reveling in the beauty of the sea, sand, and sky and treasuring our friendship.

When my husband came down for a second visit, I asked him to bring an abundance of freeze-dried food because I wanted to give a dinner dance. I invited the village council, about twelve men, including Almajor, and their wives. For music, I hired the village band that had played at the dedication of Habitation Amitié. The party was supposed to start at 5:00 in the afternoon and shortly after that hour, the men started showing up.

"Where are your wives?" I asked through Almajor, who spoke a few works of English. But the men just shook their heads, smiling. Then I saw them. Too shy to come to my house, the women were hiding out with neighbors, peeking around trees, loitering on the beach. I went after one of the youngest and prettiest and literally dragged her, protesting, to my terrace. After a few minutes, however, her shyness faded and she started having fun. Thereupon all the other women came out of hiding and joined us. We were making social history since a dinner dance with couples was unknown in Labadi.

But when I served the buffet supper—a dishpan full of cooked meat and vegetables from my freeze-dried stores, with a matching pan of rice, a tray of bananas and papayas, and a tray of cookies—the habits of a lifetime claimed the day. There was a mad stampede to the tables and in a matter of seconds the food was consumed, as if taken in one huge gulp. Living on the edge of starvation all their lives had eliminated any possible "manners" that my guests had attempted to learn at the last minute.

That was the reality of life at Labadi, as I wrote in the conclusion of my *Geographic* story:

> *My pleasure in living at Labadi cannot erase, however, my distress at being unable to alleviate the poverty surrounding me.*
>
> *Take what seems at first simply fair play in the game of curiosity: I spend the day observing the people of Labadi; they claim the night for looking at me and my husband, who has come for a visit.*
>
> *We dine by candlelight on our porch, shielded as it is from the sea wind. We are an island of light and we are on stage. All the neighbors come out for the show. Children take front-row, ground-level seats; adults stand behind.*
>
> *There is much talking and laughter until we sit down to dinner. Then the audience grows quiet, as if a curtain has gone up. And they watch with undivided attention.*
>
> *We go inside for coffee and, as if house lights had gone up, our audience begins again to visit among themselves.*
>
> *Then one night we are awakened about midnight by the sound of group singing. It comes from the home of a neighbor on the hill just behind us.*
>
> *At first the song is slow and sad, like a dirge. Sometimes the people sing it in rounds. As the night wears on, the singing gets stronger, more beautiful, like mighty chords from a great choir.*
>
> *Toward dawn, melodies come, so sweet the heart melts, and softer, evoking a sense of peace. Then silence.*
>
> *Almajor comes with the news. "A young boy died. He sick a long time."*

It is malnutrition, we learn.

And we wonder if the boy could have been one of those faces, with big wondering eyes, peering out from the dirt at the edge of light from our dinner table. And we feel an ache too sad for tears.

They take the boy's body from his home, a one-room dirt-floored dwelling that had been cleared of furniture and draped in white cloth. With family and friends we follow the coffin to the church, where the priest's helper reads a service for the dead. Afterward we climb the mountain to a cemetery so poor there are no tombstones.

A guitar picks out the plaintive strains of "Auld Lang Syne" and it is over, we think. But there is something yet to happen.

Nine days after the burial, we are sitting on our terrace, packed and ready to leave Labadi. Several neighbors walk by, nod and pass on; they carry freshly cut leafy boughs like wands. At the still-shrouded house of the dead boy, they stop and enter.

Inside they pin their green offerings to the white cloth, making a bower. In it, they sing once more, through the night. Thereafter it is over.

My Haitian friends have made it across one more mountain.

There was an ending to my story, however, that never got into the *National Geographic*. When I left Labadi and returned to Port-au-Prince, I wrote a circular that I asked the American Embassy to distribute for me to the other embassies in town. It read something like this: "Deluxe camping in Labadi on Haiti's beautiful north coast. Beachside concrete-floored cottage with foam rubber mattresses and clean linens. FLUSH TOILET and SHOWER BATH. Snorkel through coral wonders where Columbus sailed. $25 a week. Contact Gerard Almajor, c/o Walter Bussinius, Mt. Jolie Hotel, Cap Haïtien."

I had left my linens and kitchen supplies for the possible renters and had suggested the $25, hoping that the low price would guarantee full-time occupancy. And I had made but one request of Almajor, who would be in charge of the rentals. With the first money earned, free of expenses, build concrete latrines in the village to clean up the polluted stream that was its water supply.

When I returned to Labadi a year later, Almajor had kept his word and new latrines were in place. Whereupon I smashed a bottle of champagne against a concrete latrine wall in dedication and gave another party to celebrate such civic improvement. In the years that followed, Labadi made enough money from Habitation Amitié to build two other beach houses like it, making the village unique in being the only one in Haiti to have an income for public improvements and emergencies.

I never did become ambassador to Haiti and establish across the land a chain of Habitation Amitiés, with attached clinics run by Edith, but we did prove that with a little money, a lot of goodwill, and "something to be enthusiastic about" we could not only make ourselves happy but change for the better the lives of others as well.

Wearing Haitian patchwork shorts and hat, Carolyn interviews President Jean-Claude "Baby Doc" Duvalier. Photo by Thomas Nebbia.

CHAPTER 10

Adventure in France

When dreams come true at last, there is life and joy.
—Proverbs 13:12

ROM THAT MOMENT IN CHILDHOOD when I read Stevenson's *Travels with a Donkey in the Cévennes,* I wanted to retrace his journey, just as he walked it, through the mountains of southern France with a donkey as a companion.

As a reporter for the *New Orleans States,* I continued to dream of following in Stevenson's footsteps but at that time World War II was raging, with France occupied by the Nazis. As a substitute I went to Mexico, and, at Tasco, I bought a donkey and struck off from the Hotel de la Borda for a "Travels with a Burro" on the Stevenson model. I subsequently wrote a story about my adventures and sent it to the *States,* only to have it returned to me with the spelling corrected by my city editor and friendly critic, Frank Allen.

Finally, shortly after joining the staff of the National Geographic Society at age twenty-eight—just a year older than Stevenson when he took his famous walk—I proposed that the magazine send me to France to retrace the Stevenson journey. The answer was "No."

Five years later I resubmitted my proposal. Again the answer was "No." Five years later, the same thing. And five years later, the same thing. Another five years passed with another "No."

Another five years, another "No." Then, three years thereafter, I wrote the editor about my dream once again, and mentioned the fact that 1978 would be the 100th anni-versary of Stevenson's walk, a good reason for me to redo the journey in October 1977, for publication on the anniversary month a year later. At long last came "Yes." I never imagined that at age fifty-six I might be required to pull a donkey across the mountains of southern France, but when dreams come true at last there is life and joy, as the Bible says.

Carolyn and her donkey Modestine, named after Stevenson's donkey, share a moment of affection. Photo by Cotton Coulson.

From the beginning I resolved to do the journey just as Stevenson did it, walk-ing every step of the way with a donkey, over the very same terrain he walked, and camping out or sleeping in inns on the same nights he slept—only ninety-nine years later. In years past, other Stevenson admirers had walked sections of the journey alone or in company with friends. One woman had actually used a don-key for part of her trek, transporting the animal by truck over the difficult stretches. But so far as I knew, no one had ever succeeded in following Stevenson's complete route on foot and with donkey. I would be the first.

Early on I realized that a *Geographic* retracing of Stevenson's walk would, of necessity, be very different indeed from the origi-nal. Since photography was in its infancy, the young Scotsman carried no camera. He relied instead on a single, small sketchbook to record visual impressions. Because world-class photographs are the flesh and blood of the *National Geographic* magazine, we could not depend on sketches. That meant that I would not be alone on my walk with a donkey, but would be accompanied at all times by a photographer. And the photographer would be accompa-nied by the *Geographic* photographer's usual fifteen Halliburton cases of the most up-to-date photographic equipment.

Moreover, although I might pare my wardrobe and camping equipment down to the barest essentials, as Stevenson did, the photographer would require the barest essentials as well, including a sleeping bag, thus doubling our load of personal gear. We would need a whole team of donkeys to carry everything we might require. And who would manage all those animals? If Stevenson's experience with his donkey offered any insight, the management of *one* donkey would be about all I could handle.

When Stevenson sent his friend Sidney Colvin a report on his travels with a donkey, he wrote, "After an uncouth beginning, I had the best of luck to the end." In fact, my good luck began even before I left the shores of North America. Bob Gilka, director of photography for *National Geographic,* assigned a brilliant young photographer to the Stevenson story. A good-looking, curly-haired blond with beautiful manners, easy ways, boundless energy, and fluent in French, Cotton Coulson was the same age as Stevenson when he walked the Cévennes. Cotton was everything I could have hoped for, giving me every assistance when I needed it—and friendship. Of even more importance, he captured the trek in a superlative set of pictures.

I was lucky, too, in another way. When I wrote to the Club Cévenol, an organization devoted to promote tourism in the Cévennes and a prime mover in centennial observances of Stevenson's walk, I learned that the club had nearly completed marking his route in anticipation of numerous retracings throughout the centennial year. My Club Cévenol correspondant was a gentleman named Jacques Poujol, who lived in Paris but spent holidays at his family's ancestral chateau in a Cévenol village. Jacques offered help in solving our problems with so much gear. His daughter, Corinne, had gone to college in the United States where she had met and married a young American, Gordon Golding. Gordon and his wife were then living in Paris and would be free to give us a hand.

Thus it was decided. We would hire Gordon, rent a car, and pile all our clothes and equipment in it. Then, each morning as we set out on our walk, Gordon, who also was fluent in French, would go forth as our troubleshooter, making overnight arrangements for us and the donkey in the villages where Stevenson stopped, staking out campsites and lining up food where picnics were in order. In the event of an emergency, Cotton and I were linked to Gordon by walkie-talkies.

My husband, Pat, recently freed by retirement from his work as a civil servant, flew over as a morale-builder for me and traveled in the car with Gordon. Corinne showed up from time to time to cheer her husband on. But, alas, Cotton's best friend, Sisse Brimberg, a charming young Dane also working as a photographer for the *Geographic,* was on a magazine assignment halfway around the globe. Cotton found solace in placing daily telephone calls to her, some of which actually went through.

Stevenson walked 120 miles in twelve days, from the town of Le Monastier to St. Jean du Gard. His donkey, named Modestine, carried his sleeping bag and food. In his search for adventure, Stevenson yearned to come down off "this feather-bed of civilization, and find the globe granite underfoot and strewn with cutting flints."

There wasn't much doubt that he succeeded in finding some granite underfoot and cutting flints. Yet, he was much more fortunate than I in that he was able to walk country roads that were innocent of hard surfacing and free of the huge trucks and speeding automobiles that make the present-day Cévenol roads life-threatening to all foot travelers. Fortunately, Club Cévenol had marked alternate but parallel routes that avoided motorized traffic—back lanes, cattle and sheep

Modestine stands still to provide a base for Carolyn's map on their first day of walking in Stevenson's footsteps. Photo by Cotton Coulson.

paths, horseback trails, and abandoned railroad beds. It was by following these, frequently getting lost in the process, that I suffered my share of granite underfoot and cutting flints. But I run ahead of my story.

Our little party gathered at the starting point, Le Monastier, where we were houseguests of the mayor, André Broggio, who had bought a donkey for me to travel with. With the mechanization of farming in southern France, donkeys had well-nigh disappeared from the countryside. M. Broggio had to send to Spain for mine, and I aptly named her Modestine. I went for a few practice walks with her and her rarity created a stir in the neighborhood. Modestine and I got along splendidly. She seemed to listen to what I had to say and even occasionally appeared to nod in agreement.

The people of Le Monastier, concerned about Stevenson's safety on his walk, warned him of the possibility of "sudden death in many surprising forms. Cold, wolves, robbers, above all, nocturnal practical jokers … ." No one voiced such dire predictions to me, but several thought it likely that it would take me longer to walk to St. Jean du Gard than the dozen days that Stevenson required. The reason? The Club Cévenol route, linking the villages of the Scotsman's journey, was longer and more circuitous than the main roads he followed.

Modestine balks at crossing a stream; her mistress pulls hard. Photo by Cotton Coulson.

My last night in Le Monastier was filled with misgivings, if not downright anxiety. I was not a hiker, having given up long walks in my teenage years, and Stevenson set a schedule that called for walks of up to 18 miles a day—and driving a donkey as well. I was reminded of the saying: "Don't want something too much lest you're liable to get it."

I had wanted the Stevenson walk all my life, it seemed, and now that I had it in my grasp I wondered whether I might not really be up to it. Moreover, everyone I ever knew had heard of my ambition to follow in R.L.S.'s footsteps, including all my colleagues at *National Geographic*. My agitation to get the assignment had continued over a quarter of a century! Failure was unthinkable. Yet, could I do it?

Day was just breaking when Modestine, Cotton, and I, with a few well-wishers who came along for the first hour, set off from Le Monastier on September 22, 1977, just ninety-nine years to the day after Robert Louis Stevenson. I carried a large-scale map—4 yards long and rolled up on two sticks—provided by the Geographic's cartography department. It appeared to show nearly every rock along the route.

But, as with Stevenson, the donkey proved to be the problem. No longer docile, as she had been on the practice walks, Modestine now exhibited a voracious appetite and a stubborn will to satisfy it. We stopped for a snack at every bush or patch of grass. Having learned from his book how Stevenson tried by force—various reluctant beatings—to make his Modestine go forward, I had resolved to try gentler arts of persuasion, including sugar lumps, to bend my donkey to my will. But from the beginning she, not I, was in control, stopping and starting at will, walking at her own pace, and feasting on roadside vegetation whenever the mood struck.

My first disagreement with Modestine came within 10 minutes of the start: She refused to cross a shallow stream of water no wider than 4 feet. I pushed and shoved. I crossed the stream and pulled with all my might on the rope attached to her halter. I lured her with sugar lumps. I patted her tenderly and whispered endearments in her long, floppy ears. Then, after what seemed an eternity, Modestine made her own decision and, with obvious distaste, stepped gingerly across the water.

There were other differences. Modestine, for example, loved to fairly run up hills, dragging me behind, breathless and frantic

The two walkers make progress on the more-than-120-mile, twelve-day trek ... but slowly. Photo by Cotton Coulson.

in a search for safe footing amid loose stones or crumbling banks of earth. On the other hand, when going downhill, a direction easy for me to navigate and one I hoped would help us make up for lost time, Modestine showed a vast reservoir of timidity, even fear, and moved in slow motion, delicately picking each step with the greatest care and stopping often to survey the route. Until I got used to Modestine's ways, I lived with heart-sinking frustration, being so committed to sticking to Stevenson's schedule at all cost.

In time, however, I not only adjusted to Modestine's pace, but used the time to my advantage by taking notes. Of our second day on the road from Le Bouchet St. Nicolas to Langogne, I wrote in my journal:

> *No living soul walks our way, or any way. Only the cows and horses speak to us, or rather to Modestine, who is such a curiosity that the animals run from great distances across the pastures just to watch her pass. Modestine helps to satisfy their curiosity by stopping often to satisfy her passion for thistles, which she devours whole—prickles, blossoms, branches, and all.*
>
> *As for me, I have found an extraordinary new awareness of the land and animals, opened by the pace of walking. I feel that I am literally seeing everything for the first time. Cows? How fabulous they are, swinging bags of milk with little spouts, and kind eyes ... . Horses? How was it that I never saw before how aristocratic they look ... .*

But the horses and cows met along the way were not the only creatures fascinated by this rare beast, a donkey. In the villages and towns, excited children popped up from nowhere. In one village I stopped to let the kids inspect the donkey. To demonstrate her docility, I let her suck my fingers following a sugar treat. "Suddenly," as I recorded, "Modestine's great jaws closed, catching my little finger in their painful vise, drawing blood." The children were even more delighted with the mishap.

Although Modestine and I shared many a tricky moment on our climb up and down mountains, the most dangerous came when we were crossing an abandoned railroad bridge over the Mimente River, now shorn of guardrails. While the roadbed seemed solid when we began, near the end Modestine spied some holes that revealed the swirling waters of the river far below. The donkey stopped dead in her tracks. Since she wouldn't go forward, I gingerly turned her around on the narrow span. Whereupon Modestine bolted. With the strength of terror I threw myself across her neck. An eternity later, she slowed down and we walked back off the bridge.

In the end, Modestine and I came to have a high regard for one another. Given the fact that she was stronger and bigger than I, my fourteen-year-old companion could have been a tyrant. Instead, I thought she was rather sweet, with a talent for listening. At the end of our trek, at St. Jean du Gard, I made a crown of fresh carrots and radishes for her to wear and snack on during a parade through the town. She was the hit of the season.

Stevenson, too, grew fond of his Modestine and even shed tears after selling her at St. Jean du Gard. Of course, I was sad to part with my donkey. We had been through a lot together. But like the trooper she was, Modestine had other shows to star in. I shipped her back to Le Monastier and Mayor Broggio, who kept her in readiness for other walkers who might be interested in faithfully re-enacting Stevenson's journey during the centennial year.

While Modestine provided much of the adventure of my walk, the people we met along the way added another component: friendship. In a part of France where the American visitor is infrequently seen and, no doubt as a result, much welcomed, I found immediate acceptance. I have never understood why travelers think the French cold and standoffish. Paris, of course, is a big city and shares with other big cities a penchant for reserve and a love of hard-to-come-by privacy. In the Cévenol, where the population is much diminished by a flight to the cities, visitors are regarded as personal guests and accorded unusual courtesy.

Reliving the travels of the twenty-seven-year-old Stevenson proved arduous indeed for the fifty-six-year-old author. Photo by Cotton Coulson.

As for Cotton, Modestine, and me, we approached celebrity status since most Cévenols who dwell alongside the Stevenson route knew the Stevenson story and the donkey was a sure tip-off that we were reliving it. In the morning on the first day, we stopped to ask a middle-aged man for directions. He quickly identified us as Stevensonians and happily joined us as a guide for part of the way.

He looked like the farmer he was, in rough country clothes, muddy boots, slouch hat, and a stubble of a beard. But Albert du Lac de Fugères was also a nobleman, head of a family that had lived in Fugères for 800 years. He took his baccalaureate in Greek at the University of Le Puy and could quote Shakespeare in English. But his pride and pleasure lay in what distinguished his own small piece of the planet from other places.

As we strolled along, he began to sing and then to dance a Cévenol folk song and dance called a *bourrée*. Later, over luncheon at the Hôtel de la Loire in Goudet, my new friend recited an epic poem written in Occitan, the ancient language of southern France. His eyes brimming with emotion, the nostrils of his Roman nose flaring, Albert du Lac exemplified a man with love fulfilled—for his people, for his land, and for his language.

I never got the name of the Wonder Woman of Langogne, whom I first met in a state of dazed exhaustion after having walked an everlasting 18 miles over an interminable 13 hours. As desk clerk, she checked us in at the Bel Air, a country inn with modern comforts. Then, switching to her role as porter, she insisted on carrying our bags up to our rooms. When we came down for an aperitif, Wonder Woman was tending bar. Thereafter, she was the lone waitress at a dinner that, no doubt, she had cooked earlier. The next morning, there she was in cap and apron, cleaning the bedrooms and neatening up the public rooms. Cheerful and smiling, Wonder Woman was all things to everyone at the Bel Air.

Possibly as compensation for such overwork, Wonder Woman was blessed with many animal friends who appeared to be permanent fixtures at the hotel. Throughout the morning, the four chairs in the lobby were occupied by three large dogs and a puppy, two asleep, two watchful, all completely at home. When the hotel guests—there were several besides ourselves— appeared on the scene, the visitors settled for standing rather than disturbing the dogs.

Occasionally a dog would rise and, without so much as a bark, escort a guest to his room or to the dining room. At lunchtime, we were gratified to be so honored. Other dogs arrived with luncheon guests from the town and sat, with perfect manners, beside the chairs of the people they owned, dining off treats dropped from the tables. One diner was accompanied by a huge Great Dane that, even when seated on the floor, was eyeball to eyeball with his human companion. Wonder Woman, heavily laden with trays of food, moved around this living obstacle without batting an eye. Hotel dogs and guest dogs treated one another with measured indifference.

Another crowd of hotel pets were the felines. I counted two Siamese cats, two black cats, and a gray kitten, all of whom preferred to sleep on tables in the dining room until mealtimes, when they gathered atop a table of their own to feast on leftovers, scraped off the diners' plates by Wonder Woman. Their lapping and smacking created a little ripple of sound—background music as sweet and reassuring as a purr.

We followed Stevenson's lead in allowing ourselves the luxury of staying in Langogne until after lunch, but we also shared with him the trial of rain throughout the afternoon. That was the third day out, where we got lost, walked in circles, and were imprisoned by barbed wire, a cross-country walking hazard unknown to Stevenson and his Modestine. It was also the opening of the French hunting season and the countryside was filled with the unnerving sound of nearby gunshots.

By the time Cotton had found us a way out of the barbed-wire traps, night had fallen. With lanterns in hand we walked on through a ghostly fog until we reached the Mourgue farm near Fouzilhac, a village so inhospitable to Stevenson that he was forced to make camp in the darkness, with no water or proper food.

Gordon had arranged for us to sleep in the Mourgues' barn, but when we arrived wet and dead tired, the family insisted that we dry out, warm up, and picnic in their living room, an unexpected, unstinting hospitality. Uncorking bottles of wine, we and the Mourgues—father, mother, and seven offspring, the four eldest university graduates—filled the house with laughter and rapid-fire conversation in French between our host family and Gordon and Cotton. Ignorant of the language but loving the sound of it, Pat and I entered into the spirit of the affair with delight. It was so wonderfully French—and all a fitting prelude to the end of the day. We crawled into our warm sleeping bags in a barn filled with the aroma of new-mown hay and fell asleep in an instant.

Another interlude of memorable hospitality came a few days later in the valley of the River Tern, still lined with the "noble trees … unconquerable chestnuts" that Stevenson saw. After scaling Mounts Goulet and Lozère, we had entered what the Scot had called "the Cévennes of the Cévennes," a land filled with the romance of a lost cause. In the eighteenth century, the Camisard War erupted when French Huguenots rose up against Catholic prohibitions against their freedom to travel, advance their fortunes, and worship God as they pleased. France's Sun King, Louis XIV, used savage force in an attempt to stamp out the heresy.

In the village of La Vernède, we were invited by an elderly widow, Madame Turc, to picnic in her garden, which commanded a sweeping view of the river and surrounding hills. Gordon turned up with chilled white wine, cheeses, sausages, French bread warm from the oven, and fresh strawberries. We invited Madame Turc to join us.

With a wave of her hand toward the hills, Madame Turc said to me: "Battleground in the war." Of course I knew what she meant. The Camisard War is still fresh and reminded me of how the American Civil War is yet regarded in parts of the U.S. South. Sitting in that garden, sprinkled with the gold of autumn's flowers, we looked out over history as Madame Turc told us of the misery and courage, deprivation and religious fervor, that kept an old war alive.

As her treat, Madame Turc offered coffee, and when I thanked her, she demurred, "You do not have to say thank you for so little." But it was no small thing she had given us. Besides memorable hospitality, she had opened a window on her life and shared what she treasured in memory.

On the twelfth and last day of the walk we did, indeed, successfully navigate the "granite underfoot" of a steep, rocky wilderness to arrive safely and gratefully in another garden—the country home of Madame Léon Van de Putte-Latham. She welcomed us with cool water, a chair beneath her grape arbor, and a philosophical conversation that would have delighted Stevenson, who spent many hours of his trek talking religion with those he met along the way.

Madame Van de Putte-Latham showed me a book she was reading in English, *A Course in Miracles* by the Foundation for Inner Peace. She told me that, as a kind of personal atonement, she was working to help the elderly find contentment in old age.

This rewarding encounter, near the end of so arduous a trek, moved me deeply. As I confided to my journal:

> *It seems to me that I have, like Christian in The Pilgrim's Progress, attained a goal of the spirit with Celestial City on the horizon. If I came off the "featherbed of civilization" for the walk, I am not unhappy to now return to it. And yet, amid the "granite underfoot" and "cutting flints," the walk has given me time to discover how full of news the earth is. I have been witness to nature's endless parade of events—a leaf turns yellow, a stone falls and breaks, a pine bough sighs—and felt the renewal of wonder.*

CHAPTER 11

Adventure in the Wild, Part 1

One may go a long way after one is tired.
—French proverb

*I*N A SENSE IT WAS ALL A MISTAKE, and the mistake was all mine. I had drifted into a celebration of my sixtieth birthday in April 1980, and I had proclaimed to all who would listen that I didn't mind being sixty at all, especially considering the alternative—to be dead. I felt in pretty good shape for sixty, eating and exercising for health, drinking for fun. My husband was still my best friend and our two kids, now grown and more or less on their own, were a pleasure to be around. My job as a *Geographic* editor was still rewarding, with most of the early goals for it happily realized.

But shortly thereafter something began nagging in the back of my mind. Was I now out of the game? Could I still do any assignment I might want? Was I getting too *old*? God forbid! Unknown to me I had set sail on an ego trip.

A few months later I dropped by the private office of my friend Ethel Starbird, a brilliant staff writer famous for her ear for dialogue and dialect. Ethel was also famous for her hospitality and was known to pour on generous libations for her friends in after-hours bull sessions. And there, drink in hand, was Joe Scherschel, a *Life* photographer before becoming a *Geographic* star, spinning the story of what *Geographic* staffers call a "war game."

He had just returned from Tasmania, the island state of Australia, where in its uninhabited Southwest he had encountered what he considered the world's toughest terrain.

In the wilds of southwest Tasmania, Australia's island state, Carolyn and her party struggle through dense foliage. Photo by Melinda Berge.

"Talk about rough," Joe expounded, "that place has bushes that grow horizontally as tall as a man, and then turn and grow vertically. If you try to walk the matted top of that vegetation, you risk falling through to the ground several yards below, and may never be heard from again since it's almost impossible to climb out.

"And there's the Tasmanian Tiger snake, as long as my body and as big as my arm. It's deadly poisonous and there's no antidote. Not long ago a young woman hiking a Southwest trail pulled off to relieve herself, was bitten, and died 2 hours later.

"The weather is out-of-sight. Storms roar in from the Indian Ocean or the Arctic Ocean and often collide. It can be freezing cold and snowing one minute and suffocatingly hot the next. Incredible!

"That country also has a wild river, the Franklin, that flows for miles through deep gorges so remote that few people have ever seen them. But it has world-class white water, according to the handful who have been down it. In fact, the Franklin is the last river of its size to go undammed in Tasmania, and the environmentalists and power company people are in a bitter battle over its fate."

As Joe talked, I hung on every word. Instantly, I knew that this was the assignment I was looking for. So tough there could be no doubt about my being in the game. I wanted to do a story on the wild Tasmanian Southwest. But *getting* a story at the *Geographic* is sometimes the hardest part.

Fortunately, the magazine was looking for a story on Tasmania. We had covered every state in Australia and it was Tasmania's turn, the very reason why Joe Scherschel had been sent to Tasmania. His assignment was to do a general picture coverage on the whole state, but the inhabited sections had come off too tame and the story had been dropped. I immediately started sending memos on how we should cover the wild Southwest and make an adventure story out of it.

I sold the story concept to the editor and the planning council, a body composed of all the editors and department heads, whose duty was to play sounding board for ideas. But I did not sell myself as the author. Bob Gilka, director of photography, who earlier had been my photographer-partner on a story about walking New Zealand's Milford Track, was dead opposed to my going—and said so. Joe Judge, associate editor in charge of text, was lukewarm. And so was Bill Garrett, the editor, who would make the final decision as to who got the assignment.

"Hell, Carolyn," Bill said to me, "why do you want to go knock your brains out in a place like that? Why don't you pick somewhere comfortable? Come up with a European subject, where the food and wine are good. Then go and have some fun while you work."

Bill said just about everything he could think of to talk me out of Tasmania, except that I was too old to go. He never would have said that, bless him.

To bolster my case, I started walking 3 miles to work from the St. Alban's School pool, where I swam a half mile every morning, down Massachusetts Avenue to Geographic Headquarters. And I wore a backpack filled with an ever-increasing load of books to strengthen my muscles for heavy loads. I planned to be ready when and if I got the assignment.

After about a year of tending the Tasmanian flame, I found a powerful ally in Jan Ralph, then chief of photography exhibits for the United Nations in New York and a professional highly regarded by *Geographic* illustrations people. Jan was a native of Tasmania, and his parents and younger brother, Robert, were still living there. At the suggestion of my friend Tom Smith, the *Geographic's* illustrations editor and one of my few supporters for the Tasmanian assignment, I drove to New York to meet Jan and get his advice as to how to proceed.

It turned out that Jan was looking forward to going home that winter—which was summer in Tasmania—and walking the Southwest trails with his brother. Jan enthusiastically invited me to join forces with them, reassuring me that I would be up for such an expedition.

And I, in turn, invited Jan to come to Washington and, over lunch, speak to Bill Garrett and the other editors as to the safety of the adventure and my suitability to participate. He turned in a convincing performance. Thereafter, the assignment was mine and I made plans to go to Australia.

Curiously, as soon as I got the assignment, I began to feel a sense of unease, even dread, and was reminded again of the old saying that one had best not want something too much, lest one actually get it. Would I survive this toughest of all trips? Pat and I spent a long weekend together in Palm Springs, California, and he came to Los Angeles to wave me off on the plane to Australia. I'll never forget the picture of him standing forlornly at the airport security check-in, and I walking, just as forlornly, away from him down a long corridor, stopping at intervals to turn and wave at his ever-diminishing figure.

What did I have to prove at this stage in my career, I wondered, heartsick at being so foolish as to put my life in jeopardy. Who did I have to prove it to? The only answer I could come up with was: myself.

The Geographic team, photographers David Hiser and Melinda Berge and I, checked into the new Wrest Point Hotel in Hobart, the capital of Tasmania. A circular building with skyscraper aspirations, the Wrest Point represented the very pinnacle of civilization to me on stays between my several forays into the wilderness.

On Bob Ralph's recommendation, we hired Mark Clough, a young Tasmanian environmentalist, to be our guide for the adventure that we expected to last 12 to 14 days. We would hike through Tasmania's Southwest National Park, first on the South Coast Track going from east to west, then on the Port Davey Track, running northeast—an overall distance of about 100 miles as the bird flies. But, as I would shortly discover, mileage meant nothing on a route that was virtually endless on a step-by-step basis, one that led through cloying mud and dense brush, along twisting, steep, scarcely discernible trails.

With the Ralph wives, Vicky and Mary, cheerfully lending a hand—but expressing no desire to accompany us—the expedition began to get organized. Since we would encounter no grocery stores along the way, we would have to carry all the food required to feed six people for a week. An equal amount would be air-dropped to use at the start of the Port Davey Track. As a consequence, we bought what seemed like a mountain of food: trail mix (called "scroggin" by the Aussies), dried milk, dried fruits, freeze-dried meats and vegetables, coffee, and tea. The food weighed about 60 pounds and each of us was expected to carry 10 pounds of the community supplies.

I bought a three-man tent for myself, equipped with a built-in nylon floor and a zipper to lock out wild intruders, such as the Tasmanian tiger snake. I also purchased a small plastic baby potty for my use during nighttime calls of nature. I equipped it with a plastic, gold-embossed shower cap from the fancy Wrest Point Hotel and a zip-lock bag for carrying it in my

Shouldering her tent, Carolyn prepares to camp out on a beach beside the Indian Ocean. Photo by David Hiser.

backpack. My final special equipment was a Sony Walkman with some Gustaf Mahler tapes to help relieve any potential on-the-trail tedium.

The day before D-Day, we met to pack the collected gear in the basement of Bob's home, high up on the slope of Mount Wellington above Hobart. I had cut personal belongings to the bone, but even so, my pack was enormous, what with a parka, tent, sleeping bag, sleeping pad, eating/cooking kit, and my share of the food. After packing, each of us stepped onto a scale to see what we weighed. I couldn't even lift my pack, much less hoist it to my back. When my friends did it for me, I thought my knees would buckle. Staggering to the scales, I stepped on to read my weight plus 49 pounds. Not even does the U.S. Army send soldiers out with 49-pound packs!

But I dared not complain. The story and expedition had been *my* idea: I had talked *myself* into this chance to pack 49 pounds across a wilderness. And besides, when I saw the packs that our photographers David, a gentle giant of a man, and Melinda, a tall and strong woman, were preparing to carry, I could only wonder at the limits of endurance. What with cameras, lenses, film, tripod, and other essential equipment in addition to camping and personal gear, David weighed in at an extra 79 pounds, with Melinda shouldering not much less. The Ralphs were similarly heavily loaded.

That night I wrote a new codicil to my will and penned farewell letters to be delivered in case of death to Pat and the kids, Rick and Landa. I also wrote Gil Grosvenor, president of the National Geographic Society, entrusting my family to his care. I went to bed about midnight and awoke at 4 A.M. Unable to sleep, I called the night manager of the hotel and asked him to open the swimming pool, where I swam an hour—last-minute training.

At 7 A.M., with Vicky and Mary as our drivers, we piled into our cars with all the gear and drove 4 hours to the Cottle Creek start of the South Coast Trail. Then, with packs on back, we posed beside the jump-off sign, bravely smiling.

As I wrote in my *Geographic* story:

*We set off for the South Coast Track from Recherche Bay, named
for the frigate of French Adm. Bruni d'Entrecasteaux, who
precisely charted Tasmania's southern coast in 1792. We quickly
left behind all vestiges of civilization and encountered land as
raw and wild as the French found. Towering eucalyptus trees,
many bare and ghostly white from the ravages of fire. Soggy
plains of spiky button grass. Soaring, jagged peaks of distant
mountains. Stretches of rare, temperate rain forest with leatherwood, myrtle, sassafras, and beech trees, huge ferns, and a scrub
wood known as horizontal ... .*

It was not too bad except that I was tottering under all that
weight and my food pack, stashed at the top of my pack, started
sliding around. I put on my Sony Walkman
and tuned into Gustaf Mahler's Fourth
Symphony. A little music drug, I thought,
would make it *all* endurable. It was the only
time I walked the Tasmanian wilderness
with music. For I had discovered that a drug
of any kind—even music—interferes with
the concentration needed to do a nearly impossible job. We stopped at a creek to refill
water bottles and lunch on scroggin and
cheese. After 15 minutes we were pushing
on down the trail again, the weight of my
pack becoming more oppressive with every
step. A warm day, I was drenched with
sweat and longed for the sea, always a refreshment to me and where we planned to
camp for the night.

We could hear the sea long before we
saw it, but when it and a great white strand
of sand finally came into view we discovered that we were, alas, at the top of a sandy

*Shark-infested waters of the Indian Ocean
border the trail used by the author and her
party. Photo by Melinda Berge.*

cliff. I tumbled down its face to collapse on the beach. It was late afternoon and, except for a lunch break, we had walked 5 hours. A fine day's work, I thought, pleased and proud that I had endured and behaved reasonably well.

Then came the Australian understatement. We would camp at the other end of the beach, Mark declared, "just a bit farther." The "bit" involved another little "scramble" over an immense jumble of boulders, torn from the now rocky headland by winter storms. I began the perilous passage over the huge stones, never sure when the pack was going to throw me off balance and cause me to fall, breaking whatever. Then the going got truly tough. We had to scale a rock wall up to a breach in it. To go through the saddle we had to off-load the packs and pass them by hand up to the top and down. (Recall that I couldn't even lift my pack only a day before.) Jan and Bob Ralph stood by to help me and wait for me—the obvious slow one. But the heat had become unbearable and, fearful of passing out, I stopped to rest after the "scramble" and urged the Ralphs to push on.

The campsite was at the end of another long curve of beach— a hell of a distance it seemed to me—and I trudged on alone with every step an agony. At 7 P.M., 8 hours after the jump-off, I joined my companions beside the South Cape Rivulet, sank to my knees, then sprawled, motionless, for half an hour. I felt dizzy and found it hard to breathe.

But I did regain my voice in time to object to Mark's suggestion that we camp not on the beach but in the nearby woods. In the woods! That's where the Tasmanian tiger snakes lived and I wanted no part of an accidental meeting. Besides, I loved the sound of water lapping the shore and wanted to go to sleep soothed by such music. Mark finally agreed to camping on the beach. I was to learn later, much to my distress, why Mark had wanted the group to camp in the woods, but he gave no reasons at the time.

As I lay in the sand, pondering my situation, it seemed to me that everyone was embarrassed at my collapse. Perhaps, more than embarrassed, worried. David was busy with his equipment, Melinda and the Ralphs were putting up their tents, and Mark was cooking dinner. My inability to keep up was a clear liability to the expedition. With food limited, there could be no extra trail days spent waiting for me. There was no convenient hotel or family to take me in should I falter. The awesome Ironbound Range, reputed to be the most punishing traverse of the route, was only a day ahead. The South Cape Rivulet was my last chance to turn back. For the sake of the others, I felt I had no choice but to walk out the next day the way I had come, and let the others continue on schedule.

Just before dinner, Melinda helped me put up my tent; I didn't bother to stake it since the night was serene, the stars glorious. I ate lightly, announced my decision to turn back the next day, and crawled into my tent and the comfort of my sleeping bag. I fell asleep instantly.

Sometime in the night a call from nature awakened me. And in the privacy of my own tent, I broke out my plastic potty, relieved myself, covered the pot with my gold-embossed shower cap, and went back to sleep.

Again I awoke, this time to the terrifying scream of wind. Coming out of nowhere and without warning, a howling, raging storm, full of pelting rain, attacked without mercy. My tent, unstaked, threatened momentarily to become airborne. Only my body and heavy pack anchored it, however tenuously. But the contents of the plastic potty, by no means contained by a flimsy shower cap, flew free, generously sprinkling the walls of my new tent, fouling my new sleeping bag, dappling my new backpack. Shame and embarrassment over this new disaster drowned any fear of the storm.

I switched on my flashlight, found my single roll of toilet paper, and began frantically to clean up. Then, unzipping my front "door," I dug a hole in the sand just outside with my plastic hand trowel and buried the wet toilet paper, a whole roll of it.

Thereafter, I went outside and, bending against the unceasing wind, staked my tent. I learned later that had we camped in the woods, the trees would have broken the force of the wind and the storm, a frequent visitor in these parts, would have left us largely unaffected—the reason why Mark had opted for a protected campsite.

Bob and Jan, it was oddly comforting to see, had also failed to stake their tent, which would have flown away had not Mark, sleeping outdoors, caught it. Melinda and David, sharing a tent, appeared to have slept through the storm. David, it seems, had taken the precaution of staking their tent before retiring. I resolved to watch David in the future.

And there would be a future, I swore, since my single failure appeared to be the inability to carry such a great weight. I would go back to Hobart, hire someone to help me, and return to the expedition.

Jan and Mark insisted on walking me out the next morning, with plans to return in the afternoon and try to catch up with others at Granite Beach, the ongoing next campsite. They left their packs at the Rivulet so that they could carry my pack on the walk out; they also carried out some 50 pounds of gear suddenly deemed unnecessary by the others, who, like me, had suffered from too heavy a load.

With only a light day-pack on my back, I had my first chance to really appreciate the scenery: immense virgin beaches of white sand and dramatic rock formations carved by the sea—one, called Lion's Head, as majestic as the Sphinx. We easily made the walkout in less than 3 hours. A pleasure.

The author slogs down a muddy path in Tasmania's wild southwest. Photo by David Hiser.

At Cottle Creek, we lucked into a park ranger who drove us to the farthest south telephone in Australia—Lune River—where I called Hobart and ordered a helicopter sent. It landed on an emergency pad near us, and we all climbed aboard to return to the Rivulet where Jan and Mark picked up their packs. Then the helicopter dropped the two men at Granite Beach, to await the arrival of our party, still on the trail. As for me, I went back to Hobart in the helicopter and began looking for the help that would enable me to return to the wilderness.

Victoria Sandford, a strong, athletic young woman in her early twenties, turned out to be just what I was looking for. She had tramped the Southwest on several occasions and was knowledgeable about the plants and animals we might encounter along the way. Moreover, she was easy to live with, an important consideration since we would be sharing my three-man tent and walking together.

I booked another helicopter ride and Victoria and I flew off to the rendezvous with the hiking party at Cox Bight. That night, around the campfire, I heard tales of trial and triumph in the climbing of the Ironbound Range. Jan Ralph's diary tells the story:

> *The tract is very muddy and steep and we begin the mode of march that will become routine. You constantly have to step up, raising one foot about the knee level of the other each time as the track ascends in an ever-increasing gradient. We maintain a very good pace but the breathing is heavy and labored from the severity of the effort.*
>
> *During the second hour we come into the steepest trail yet. I can describe it in one word—brutal! We climb over fallen trees with large root systems. The constant rain up here creates pools of water and mud and if you misstep you can find your leg up to the knee in clinging, glutinous mud. Sometimes you become tipped over into the mud by the weight of your pack.*

Though sick with stomach cramps and diarrhea, Jan still appreciated the beauty. The next day, still in the Ironbound Range, he wrote:

The view from the western rim is so magnificent that I forget my problems. The sky is brilliantly clear and you can see at least 60 miles in any direction. Staggering views. Wild forests, deep valleys, enormous mountain range stretching inland. The coastline is dramatic in both directions and, to top it off, we see a pod of whales out at sea. This one view makes the whole effort worthwhile.

After our night at Cox Bight, we sloughed across a muddy valley to Melaleuca and moved into huts built for bush walkers as a memorial to Charles King by his son, Denny, one of the half dozen people who live in the Southwest National Park. The Kings, father and son, started tin mining around Cox Bight in the 1930s. After service in World War II, Denny returned to take up mining leases near Moth Creek where he built a home with his own hands, calling it Melaleuca after a native tree and thus giving the area its name.

We were all anxious to meet the King of the Southwest since he was one of a kind: a survivor in a wilderness where few have remained for long.

Among Europeans, the convicts came first in 1821, condemned to a living hell at Macquarie Harbour. Until the prison closed in 1834, the doomed men worked under the lash to cut the venerable Huon pine, which can grow as long as 2,000 years, and build ships with its matchless timbers. Most who tried to escape died miserably in the impenetrable rain forest.

In the 1850s Port Davey attracted whalers and sealers, to be followed by the "piners" harvesting the Huon. But the gold rush around Tasmania's Queenstown in the late 1800s emptied the Southwest of its live-in adventurers. A half century later maps still showed huge blank areas as "unexplored."

Residing in the heart of that wilderness, Denny King has nevertheless managed to create an island of comfort and culture. We met with him over steaming cups of coffee and cake still warm from the oven as a wood fire dispelled the chill of a rain-driven, wind-tossed night.

Short, wiry, and strong for his age, Denny talked of his work as a miner and weather reporter, of his pastimes, photography and painting, of his books, and of his travels. He had just returned from a 15-day hike in the Himalaya and hoped to visit Patagonia soon.

Denny had the companionship of his daughter Mary, the joy of his four-year-old granddaughter Kyle, and the help of Annie Ball, a young woman from Perth who was interrupting her career as an architect to spend a year working in the wild.

He also had the delight of coaxing a bounty from a nature perverse in these parts. The often-gusting wind drove the generator that lighted his house. The ever-ready rain supported a garden that yielded raspberries, gooseberries, youngberries, cherries, plums, apples, tomatoes, peas, beans, turnips, potatoes, zucchini, lettuce, and parsley.

And through it all, Denny enjoyed the blessing of a sense of humor. Taking us across Bathurst Harbour in his boat, he remarked on the brownish water stained by tannin from the shore-lining peat.

"A visitor once asked me why the water was colored that way," Denny said, "and I told her we had been dumping our tea leaves in it." His bushy eyebrows lifted to express the whimsy as a smile transformed his face.

We bade Denny good-bye at Farrell Point and started up the Port Davey Tract, first cut to give shipwrecked sailors a way out of the wilderness. Climbing up Lindsay Hill, we looked into the very face of Mount Rugby. On the few occasions when it doffed its caps of clouds, the bare white pate of the quartzite mountain showed through threadbare hairs of green.

As I wrote in my *Geographic* story:

We marched into fairy-tale glens of scaly-bark tea trees, as shaggy as sheepdogs. Shedding, the dense stands spread smooth brown carpets on the forest floor. We pushed across creeks, sometimes walking over logs, sometimes swinging off boughs, sometimes balancing on slippery rocks, sometimes just wading.

We climbed forested slopes that were almost vertical, with mud-slick roots for foot and hand holds. We descended on tracks so steep that ultimately I lost four toenails. We sank in mire up to our knees. ...

We often tramped in pouring rain, seeing nothing but our feet and the step ahead. Once I asked David whether he thought pictures in wet weather would be informative. "Yes," he replied, "of sheer suffering."

We hit the exposed Lost World Plateau in a rare dry interlude, and our eyes opened to the immensity of the wildscape, where we could almost see forever. At Watershed Camp late that afternoon the waning sun inspired Melinda and me to take a bath in the cold waters of the trailside creek. Clean, dry, and back in the tent, I noticed what appeared to be a black twig resting on my hand, and I gave it a brush only to discover it was attached.

"That's a leech," Victoria explained. In revulsion, I tore the worm off my hand, leaving a wound that bled for 4 hours—a forerunner of what was to come.

A morning-long rain began at dawn the next day, hitherto known in our crowd as Leech Day. Leeches on the brush through which we had to pass attached themselves to us like a plague, crawling under trousers and gaiters, down into socks, under shirts. We had regular leech breaks, stopping to peel off clothes and pick off the pests. And with each bite, the blood would flow for hours. Blood from bites on the legs soaked our socks, giving each step a slurpy sound.

And from my *Geographic* report:

Fine weather the next day opened to us the best views of the awesome crags of the Arthur Range, rising suddenly and sheer from the Crossing River Valley. Then after so much beauty, our eyes were assaulted by the immense barren cut on the earth left by the construction of Scotts Peak Dam, at the northern end of the Port Davey Track. We looked down on the drowned Lake Pedder, with its one-of-a-kind white sand beach, now lost forever beneath reservoir waters.

At the end of the Port Davey Track, or the beginning for those who might start their trek into the wilderness at that point, some wag had erected a gallows with a swinging rope. A sign attached to it invited all who would walk the Track to take the easy way out and hang themselves before their troubles began.

We laughed knowingly. But the sentiment had too much truth in it to be much of a joke. I had lost 17 pounds on the hike. But I had survived, thanks to Victoria's help in backpacking the gear. And she would continue to help me when, with Melinda and Annie Ball, I returned to the South Coast Track to cover those sections I had missed at the beginning of the expedition.

From that last week back on the South Coast Track, my diary recorded more rain, more mud, and a hailstorm that turned the ground white. There was one pretty day when I swam off Osmiridium Beach, unaware that

A log is the only bridge across this Tasmanian stream. Photo by Melinda Berge.

the waters were shark infested. At our last campsite, on Prion Beach, I came face-to-face with the deadly tiger snake, standing guard over the single level beachside spot where we might have pitched our tent. Without hesitation we elected to camp instead on the rain-saturated slope of the mountain trail.

The last day, the helicopter we ordered to pick us up on Prion Beach swirled in through a sleet and snowstorm, at considerable risk to its safety. And from the intrepid young pilot, concerned to get us out before the predicted really bad weather arrived, we learned to our horror that rescue teams were at that moment working the coast to find the body of a man taken by a shark.

That night at the Wrest Point Hotel I slipped my aching body into a deep hot bath and considered that I was experiencing a bit of heaven on earth. There is nothing like the pleasure that comes when the pain stops.

CHAPTER 12

Adventure in the Wild, Part 2

I like terra firma—the more firma, the less terra.
—George S. Kaufman

I BEGAN MY *GEOGRAPHIC* STORY ON TASMANIA with a tribute to the Franklin River:

> *The river, as wild and beautiful a torrent as any on the face of the planet, picked its course eons ago and began its masterwork. On the body of the land it probed and sliced, cut, shaped, and carved, sculpturing the chasms and canyons that now glorify its passage. And it added an everlasting roar in celebration.*

Even so, I might have missed it because almost everyone in Tasmania, especially my friends in the Wilderness Society, urged me not to make the arduous 12-day run through rugged uninhabited country, most of which was inaccessible except from the river. No one mentioned my sixty years but I learned that, as far as was known, I would be the oldest woman to attempt to travel the full length of the river. Once again I reviewed my will and added a few extra lines to letters to the family and National

Low water level and a chaos of rocks make the passage down the wild Franklin River truly perilous. Photo by David Hiser.

Geographic Society President Gil Grosvenor to be delivered only in the event of my demise. Even so, I was determined to go. I had gained confidence on the wilderness walk; after all, I thought, a wilderness ride couldn't be that much worse.

There were many reasons why I wanted to make the Franklin passage, but a critical one was that the Franklin River was direly threatened by a proposed hydroelectric dam. Shortly before we arrived in Tasmania the "greenies," as environmentalists there are called, staged the largest demonstration on the island since the Vietnam protests in order to dramatize what would be lost should the power project go forward. The Franklin was, in fact, the last major wild river in Tasmania suitable for power use, and the fighting over its fate was intense.

To protect the river, Australia's federal government had declared it part of the Franklin-Lower Gordon Wild Rivers National Park, a status the river enjoyed during my visit. Nevertheless, a few months after I departed Tasmania in May 1982, the Tasmanian Liberal Party came to power and its leader, Premier Robin Gray, vowed to flood the Franklin, calling it "a brown, leech-ridden ditch."

I harbored the hope that a *National Geographic* magazine account of the river's scenic wonders might be a weapon in the fight to save it. Moreover, I wanted to see for myself what was at stake, and if high adventure was a part of the trip, so be it.

Once again, we gathered in Bob Ralph's home to plan and pack. There we met the two leaders of our forthcoming river run: Martin Badham and Andy Roberts, young athletes from England. They proved quite a contrast in looks and personality. Stockily built but carrying no fat, blond and blue-eyed Martin had a large mustache and ringlets in his hair. Andy was tall, muscular, tightly wound—"a real leader and intelligent," I confided to my notebook, adding "very interesting but possibly difficult."

These were the men who would captain our two Avons, gray pontoon boats that were capacious enough to carry four people each with the necessities of life—food, tents, sleeping bags, and the bare minimum of clothes—all packed in black, waterproof rubber bags.

Besides our *Geographic* photographers, David Hiser and Melinda Berge, and the Tasmanian brothers, Jan and Bob Ralph, the party would include David Harries and Jim Bucirde. Quiet, thoughtful, highly competent, David, whom we called Davy, was getting his master's degree in environmental sciences from the University of Tasmania. Handsome Jim, a twenty-one-year-old champion canoeist, had—just barely—survived a daring attempt to canoe across Bass Strait, which separates Tasmania from the Australian mainland. Jim would paddle a small yellow raft, called a "rubber ducky," and carry the photographers' gear.

"Make no mistake," said Martin Badham, "going down the Franklin River is a very hard trip. The difficulty is not so much in the rapids, although there are some of good size and dangerous. The difficulty is in the isolation, the remoteness. There is just no help if we get into trouble."

It was the same story as the wilderness trek, but the river, we knew, would be a good deal more dangerous. Martin's warning failed to mention another serious difficulty that would assail us within minutes of launching our boats two days later. The water was devastatingly low.

The Franklin is a world-class obstacle course. Many great rafting rivers, such as the Colorado, have more-or-less stationary stone obstacles that create rapids. Only the volume of water swirling over and around those obstacles adds the unknown element and provides the challenge, as well as the hazard, of white watering.

With the Franklin there is, besides stones, a second category of obstacles—uprooted trees and stumps, limbs, and sticks—and these obstructions create yet another unknown element. Redistributed with every heavy rain or flood, the woody trash creates a new river for each party of rafters, making mastery of its 75-mile-long course almost impossible. And with a low-water level the

Franklin unveils twice as many obstacles while doubling the danger from underwater traps by bringing them closer to the surface. All this was carefully explained to us by our leaders, an enlightenment that tended to raise the level of anxiety.

My daily diary tells the story of our 12-day passage down the Franklin.

Day 1

Today I see the chaos of creation. Immense boulders tumbled from the cliffsides sit amid the ceaseless clamor of rushing water. Rock walls, vaulting skyward, undulate with the grace of immense ferns. Mighty trees, tossed like jackstraws into the river, here block, there allow, a boatwide passage. There is every size and every shape of everything at every age. And color, too. Gray, tan, pink, and beige for the rocks, brown for the tree trunks, green for foliage, and darker green where the river flows deep.

But to start at the beginning. Having driven up from Hobart, the capital of Tasmania, we eat a late lunch of fresh rye bread, butter, cheese, and corned beef near the bridge that crosses the Collingwood River, a tributary of the Franklin that we will use for a short distance on this first day before entering the Franklin. With our Avons in the water, we practice the paddle strokes that will help us follow our captains' commands—"Draw right. Draw left. Fast forward. Reverse. Spin." At last we head downstream, only to come immediately to a jarring halt atop mid-river stones and logs.

Everyone is ordered out of the Avons and into the river to manhandle the 275-pound boats, loaded with supplies, over and around the barriers. "One, two, three, move!" cry Martin and Andy to synchronize the team effort. "One, two, three, move! One, two, three, move!" Pulling, pushing, lifting, straining, the captains and crews send the boats slowly downstream, often by only inches at a time.

I can be of little help since the river's fast current and slippery rocks keep tripping me up. I feel lucky to be able to take care of myself, however, and not be a care to the others, who have their hands full. Fortunately, my life jacket and wet suit—the required dress for all—cushion me against scratches

*from frequent falls and spare me the chill of repeated
drenchings.*

*In my struggle to keep up, jumping in and out of my Avon,
crawling over logs, creeping across wet boulders, I can do little to
prevent a serious accident. Martin, waist deep in the river, loses
his footing and falls sprawling, the strong current sweeps him
downstream with brutal force, bumping him roughly against
mid-stream boulders. David, who can do anything and do it
better than most, tries to save Martin but is himself swept
downstream. David escapes harm but Martin injures his right
leg—badly. Shortly after, running the rapids at the confluence of
the Collingwood and Franklin Rivers, my friend Jan Ralph is
dumped overboard and is also swept downstream into "the most
forceful water I have ever had to contend with," as he said. He
manages to swim to shore where he sits shivering from the chilled
water and shock.*

*That night in a wooded camp on a bluff above the Franklin,
we discover a happy use for the horizontal shrub that was so
hazardous on the wilderness walk: The long tree trunks stretching out above our tents serve as convenient clotheslines for drying
wet suits.*

*Jan drops around to my tent for a visit and confides that he,
too, has put his personal papers in order before leaving Hobart, a
measure of the apprehension that he harbors about our rafting
adventure.*

Day 2

*I begin today to see the pattern of our travel. Sitting in our
Avons, we all paddle in answer to our captains' commands when
the water is sufficiently deep to carry us. Encountering shallows,
we leap out and lift the boats over the stones. When a growing
roar signals rapids ahead, Martin and Andy order us to paddle to
the riverbank and they debark. Walking down to the rapids, the
two men study the obstacles and currents like a couple of doctors
in consultation. They point to water channels, trees, rocks, and
other features, nod, disagree, ponder with brows knitting, heads
shaking.*

*If they agree on a strategy and believe the rapids safe enough
to run, they announce what water channel we take and what*

instructions we might get during the run. If they consider the risk of running too great, several options remain. The boats, free of passengers and sometimes gear to lessen the weight, might be walked over shallows or go down the rapids at the end of a line. Should this not prove feasible, there remains the option to portage, when everything—supplies AND boats—go downstream on the backs of captains and crew. EVERYBODY HATES TO PORTAGE, so backbreaking is the job.

As luck would have it, we begin this day with a portage but it isn't too bad since everything had already been unpacked for the overnight. A subsequent lining, however, is almost our undoing. We come to a spot where huge boulders had fallen into the river and the narrow water channel is clogged with swollen hulks of trees. It is decided that the gear, securely held under nylon netting, might stay aboard but each boat would have to be tilted on its side to get through the narrow passage.

This time it is Bob Ralph's turn to slip. Straining at the lower edge of his Avon, Bob loses his footing and the force of the water drives him into a huge submerged tree where his leg is caught in a "V" between its trunk and a large branch. Everyone rushes to extricate Bob before he drowns under the pounding of water. But in the urgency of the moment, Jim fails to tie up his small raft and it starts floating downstream. Quickly, Jim scales a huge boulder in mid-river, makes a breathtaking high dive, and, swimming furiously, reaches his boat just in time.

Between such perilous moments I drink in the beauty. We pass magnificent Huon pines, hundreds of years old. I had read that the piners in search of the Huon were the only people to ever go up the Franklin. They nearly wiped out the trees, so valuable as masts in sailing-ship days. Only here on the farthest reaches of the river can the old kings still be seen.

We pass beetling cliffs of sheer rock that lean out into the river, their shadowy undersides dance with light reflecting off the water—little phantoms in ballet. Walls of green moss, as curly and deep-piled as a shag rug, loom to one side while a barren cliffside provides toeholds for myrtle and gum trees, vaulting high into the sky.

The white blossoms of the leatherwood tree, so loved by Tasmanian bees that they produce a distinctive honey called leatherwood, shower our campsite, set high on a bluff. We eat a vegetable stew over noodles in almost total silence. On the basis of the evening mood, I decide that outdoor people are, by and large, quiet, stolid, and mostly humorless. Humor, I theorize, must be an urban talent since it is so necessary in dealing with people. In the wild, humor appears little needed, except by me. I ask Melinda what she thinks of my theory and she replies that humor is missing because everyone is so tired that they only want rest when getting to camp. So do I, but a laugh would help. I can see why there are no laughs from Martin, however: His knee has swollen to twice its normal size and his pain is evident.

After a swim in cold but refreshing water, I decide to sleep out under the stars and spread my sleeping bag on a rocky ledge since no rain is expected. The stars are brilliant and strange to me, but not unfriendly: One moves across the sky like a gentle wanderer on its way to worlds

A swim in a placid part of the river: a moment of relaxation at day's end. Photo by David Hiser.

unknown. The moon comes up, so full and bright that I pull my sleeping bag over my eyes. In our narrow canyon the stars are few enough to be numbered and the moon's visit is brief. I sleep fitfully since I lie on a slope and am always about to roll down the mountain, or so it seems. In my sleep I feel myself going and that awakens me. Then I shift, readjust, and drop off once again.

Day 3
We begin the day early with the river shrouded in shadow and mist and line the boats down from our cliff-top campsite. We hope to be able to run the rapids above the Irenabyss—the Chasm of Peace—but when Martin attempted a section, his boat "wrapped" a rock and was nearly swamped. Thereafter we line the boats through. At one point I fall off a slippery rock and into the swirling currents, but Jan is instantly ready with a hand to pull me out.

Late in the morning we paddle through the Irenabyss, a narrow, serpentine gorge, here and there shafted with sunlight, as

Jan Ralph pulls Carolyn to safety after she tumbles from an Avon into the turbulent Franklin River. Photo by David Hiser.

beautiful and tranquil as its name, and set up camp on one of the spacious flat rocks at the water's edge. It is an afternoon for creature comforts. Melinda and I find a secluded spot to strip and bathe. Delicious. I crawl into my sleeping bag for an afternoon nap. Luxury. This evening we watch the sunset as Jan and Bob cast for trout. Idyllic. Once again, the wilderness is teaching me to appreciate the smallest, usually-taken-for-granted things. The Irenabyss shares its peace with us, an unexpected gift from the wild Franklin.

But our sense of well-being is shortly shattered. Martin's knee is so painful and swollen that he decides to try to walk out on the Fincham Track the next day. There is discussion about the difficulty of continuing without Martin, of abandoning the Franklin run at McCall's, a track put in by the would-be dam builders. I speak privately to Jim about the two of us continuing on to the end in the rubber ducky. He agrees to help me complete the run regardless of what the others do. God willing, I shall run the length of the Franklin River!

The next day, our fourth, Martin left us to walk out on the Fincham Track. For 9 hours he hobbled, in excruciating pain, fighting off with a big stick the attacks of the deadly poisonous tiger snakes who were bold, fearless, and aggressive in the mating season.

Jim was assigned Martin's job as an Avon captain; Davy took Jim's place on the rubber ducky. Andy was now our one and only leader. We all drew closer.

A good thing, too, for on Day 5 disaster sideswiped us, twice. Running a rapid, my Avon hit a snag hidden at the bottom of the falls. Before I knew what had happened, the rear pontoon that was my seat rapidly began to sink. We had suffered a puncture and the urgency in Andy's voice—"Fast forward! Draw right! Spin! Spin! Spin!"—told me it was serious.

As we struggled toward the riverbank, the raft's stern went underwater and the heavy gear, lashed to a steel frame amidships, was suddenly in my lap, pinning my legs under the sinking craft. Andy, my partner in the stern, had managed to leap to shore, which was on his side where he, David, and Melinda hurried to secure the bow.

I felt rising fear as I fought to free my legs. Finally, ducking underwater and kicking deep, I swam free, out into the raging current, around the boat, to safety.

It takes all hands to free an Avon from its burden of water gathered during a run down a rapid. Photo by David Hiser.

It took 2 hours to repair the gash in the pontoon and a surgeon could not have been more meticulous or skilled than Andy who, far more than anyone, recognized that the boat was our lifeline to civilization.

While we waited for the patch to dry, misfortune struck once again. Bob Ralph stumbled and fell into the river from a ledge several feet above it and landed hard on solid rock. Though his foot and ankle did not appear broken, Bob could barely walk. It was painful just to see his pain.

My notes pick up the story:

> In the afternoon after the accident we paddle down to rapid after rapid but all must be lined. With backbreaking effort, the men and Melinda pull, push, tug, twist, and otherwise force-fit the loaded rafts over, under, around, through, and about the obstacles of stones, rock masses, trees, logs, and water courses. Because of the low water and Bob's incapacitating injury, our journey is more and more becoming "Mission Impossible."

My mood changed to optimism the next day, Sunday, as we paddled through the lakelike Inception Reach to the music of a choir of birds. We passed Blush Falls, a glory dropping in two columns for 100 meters down a cliff face of red stone. Clouds billowed white in a blue sky and a powerful wind came to make the reed-clad heights shimmer like a mirage.

And then we were at the Churn, the beginning of the Great Ravine where sheer cliffs, soaring to infinity, wall the river to create its most dramatic scenery.

To portage the Churn we had to scale the face of the cliff—my first experience at rock climbing. And of course we had to move the gear as well. In such an up-and-down world there was no proper campground so our party had to split up for the night. Each member had to find bodywide ledges high in the rock wall lining the river. I found a spot just level enough for my sleeping bag atop an immense boulder in the middle of the stream. As a precaution, I surrounded it with small stones that I hoped would make a clatter and awaken me if I stirred during the night and dislodged them. Not unnaturally, I had a dread of rolling off my precarious perch during the night and, as a consequence, didn't get much sleep.

But, as I wrote in my diary, the night was far from dull: "My night music was the river in full voice; my show, an hours-long parade of brilliant stars with the waning moon making a cameo appearance."

It took all of our seventh day to make five portages and as many linings through the Great Ravine. Arduous as it was, however, we felt blessed because the low water, for once, was best for the Great Ravine. High water would have dictated a day-long, cliff-top portage around Thunderrush, or we could have been marooned for days on some river ledge waiting for the water to drop.

Even so, another terror awaited us. The day of our passage through the Great Ravine turned dark at noon and the acrid smell of smoke and steady rain of ashes told the story. Forest fire! As night fell, we saw the sky turn red and the wind blow hot. The fire seemed very close, indeed. Any minute, we feared, it might leap over the crest of the surrounding mountains and sweep down to the water's edge burning everything in its path—including us.

Davy did not reassure us with his recollection of Tasmania's 1967 fire. "In 5 hours," he said, "it burned 1,000 square miles, took more than 50 lives, and left 7,000 homeless. It was called a 'descent into hell.'"

After that, I decided to sleep on the river, in the rubber ducky, reasoning that if the fire did sweep to the river's edge, I could paddle out to the middle of the stream and, perhaps, survive.

Sometime near dawn it started to rain—a welcome deterrent to the fire—and the river began to rise, promising big rapids that we might finally run. As the camp stirred to life, we learned that Bob's foot was much improved. Things appeared to have taken a turn for the better.

In Glen Calder, as I wrote, "We slipped with ease and pleasure over the first Stepped Falls, with its 3-foot drop. The second Stepped Falls, just downstream, was a more serious matter. There the water dropped 6 feet, striking an enormous rock on the right that diverted the mainstream to the left."

Seated on the starboard stern of the Avon I had learned a special stroke—paddle at my back, handle against my waist, pull hard—which was frequently called into use when Andy deemed it necessary to turn the raft to the left.

After studying the second Stepped Falls, Andy said to me, "You know, Carolyn, the problem is the rock on the right. As we go over the falls, you'll have to put in your stroke to miss the rock and turn us left."

"Yes, I know," I replied nervously.

As we paddled into the main stream and headed downriver, Andy called to Melinda on the port bow "Draw left! Draw left!" With all her considerable strength, Melinda pulled but too much.

As we sped toward the falls, Andy called again urgently. "Draw right! Draw right!" David, on the starboard bow, and I responded, but again too much, and over the brink we went in disarray. I put

Running a rapid on the Franklin, Carolyn flies from her seat at the rear (on left) of the Avon, falling into the rolling water. Photo by David Hiser.

in my stroke, but it came too late and too weak. The boat crashed against the rock, hitting it broadside near the stern. I was knocked into the air and out of the raft, but I was not without a lifeline. Flying out I had grabbed Andy's leg, and he caught, as he said, "a chunk" of me, and together we pulled me back on board to safety.

"The most beautiful portage," as I reported in the *Geographic,* "was our last, the misnamed Pig Trough. Here the river makes a huge bend, cutting away at bedrock and tumbling into its course enormous, jagged boulders. At one point the river has created a cliff-sided island topped with trees, vines, and ferns—a never-never garden from the scenery of dreams ... ."

All was contrast. Stern rocks of gray, brown, and blue, the river white with froth, spiky pandamus, lacy ferns, downy mosses, spicy evergreens, tea trees, laurel, myrtle, and the familiar horizontally growing scrub we had met earlier. And finally, there was the wispy, misty chute of a waterfall singing the melody to the river's roaring bass chords.

But beauty shortly gave way to an eyesore. At McCall's the Tasmanian Hydro Electric Commission had installed a haulage system and a pedestrian suspension bridge over the river. As Jan observed, "To see such man-made utilities after having lived with the natural order of wilderness is an assault on the senses." Yet, in the end, we had to use the bridge's anchor platforms to sleep on since the canyon was so steep there was no place to pitch a tent.

And thus we came to the lower Franklin, a broad, almost pastoral river lined with limestone caves where prehistoric humans made homes some 20,000 years ago. We ran Double Fall with the skill of veterans, or so Andy said. But we took his advice that Big Fall was beyond our powers. Alas, it was also beyond the powers of an experienced young raftsman who lost his life on a run down it the following day.

On Day 10, a cold, hours-long rain came to plague us and by nightfall we were, once again, without a proper campsite. And, once again, we were forced to use a structure put up by the Hydro Electric Commission—a filthy one-room hut. But it had a fireplace, which allowed us the pleasure of getting out of our smelly wet suits to get warm. By this time the wet suits themselves were the cause of major discomfort.

Jan spoke for us all, especially me, when he wrote in his diary:

Even though we have been living on the water, you would think that we would stay clean and fresh from the constant immersing and soaking but this is not necessarily so. Washing in the river every day is habitual but everything, including your own body, stinks of it. It is purely, simply a river smell—dank, rotting, even fetid would not be too extreme a description. Our clothes, sleeping bags, and gear all become permeated by the damp, never dry, always odoriferous stink of stagnant water.

The wet suits are a particular curse. Any water that gets inside is held against the body and warmed. It also stagnates and, with perspiration trapped inside, the odor that results is terrible. This trip is severe enough physically without the added burden of stinking as well. Bad enough for a man but horrible for a woman.

The next night, however, we had the pleasure of camping on a sandbar. And then it was over. With the rapids behind us and with the river at peace with itself, we lazily paddled and drifted down to where the Franklin flows into the Gordon River. There we arrived in time to flag down the excursion boat that sails out of Strahan daily filled with sightseers.

Once on board, we celebrated survival and lifted a glass in a toast to the Franklin. "Long may it run untrammeled by man!" we cried. Happily the Australian government felt the same way and, in the months following the publication of my story in the *Geographic,* it decreed that no dams be constructed to impede the freedom of the Franklin. I like to think that I may have played some small part in framing that momentous decision since, at the behest of the Tasmanian Wilderness Society, the Geographic Society mailed a copy of the story to each member of the Australian Parliament.

Reflecting on my experience, I remember what my friend Bob Brown, head of the Tasmanian Wilderness Society, once said of the wilderness he tries to protect: "Above all, it is an environment for finding a new kind of self, something better than the self that exists in the everyday world."

Despite the dangers and discomforts, I felt that I had been the beneficiary of that bequest of the wilderness, both on the trail and on the river. Regardless of what prompted me to go to Tasmania, I had been enriched by my days and nights in the natural world, and I was grateful.

CHAPTER 13

Adventure in the Far Pacific

Every perfect traveler creates the country where he travels.
—Nikos Kazantzakis

T ALL BEGAN WITH MY SEARCH FOR THE ISLAND OF ULUL, a mere scrap of land lost in the vastness of the Pacific, unknown to all except those few who live there, some neighboring islanders, and, of course, mapmakers. It is a part of an equally obscure atoll called Namonuito in the state of Truk, an island barely remembered from World War II days when the United States sank a Japanese fleet in its harbor. Truk is one of the four Federated States of Micronesia, in itself one of two Pacific island groups that recently became independent nations after nearly a half century as Trust Territories administered by the United States under U.N. auspices.

For my last assignment on staff, the National Geographic sent me to cover the story of those former Trust Territories, including the Commonwealth of the Northern Mariana Islands, which had opted to become part

Carolyn dives on the coral-encrusted wreck of the Japanese fleet sunk by U.S. forces in Truk harbor during World War II. Photo by David Hiser

of the United States as a territory, and the Republic of Palau, which has recently approved a constitution separating it from the United States. Accompanied by Pat, we prowled the Pacific for three months, crisscrossing an area the size of the continental United States. Mostly we went by air but for ten days we took to the sea in a ship and experienced the incredible voyage of the *Micro Dawn*.

The *Micro Dawn* was a government ship with the mission to sail out at intervals with passengers and supplies bound for the far-flung islands of Truk. In protracted negotiations, it was arranged that Pat and I would join the *Micro Dawn* on its next trip bound for Ulul and the Namonuito atoll, as well as the Western islands known as Pulap, Tamatam, Puluwat, and Pulusuk. It was promised that the voyage would only take a week, a critical factor to me since I was running out of time to complete my Pacific coverage. Besides, Ulul was a big gamble and might not yield enough story material to be worth the effort of going there.

The reason I wanted to go to Ulul was because of my admiration for the then president of the Federated States of Micronesia, Tosiwo Nakayama, who had spent several of his formative years on Ulul. What had the island contributed to the making of the remarkable man he became?

I had met President Nakayama at Kolonia on Pohnpei, the capital of the Federated States of Micronesia, and in a long interview he revealed his plans, aspirations, and appraisals of current and future courses his nation might take. I managed to draw from him the story of his life.

Prior to World War II, Nakayama's father, a Japanese businessman, was sent to work in Truk where he met and married Nakayama's mother, a young woman from the island of Ulul. Tosiwo, the lone son, and several daughters were born of their union. When war broke out, the senior Nakayama moved his family to Dublon in Truk Lagoon, headquarters of the Japanese. There the nine-year-old boy heard the "ominous, incessant, ever-louder drone" of U.S. warplanes come to sink a Japanese fleet of sixty naval and cargo vessels.

When the hostilities ended, the United States sent all Japanese nationals from the captured Pacific islands home to Japan, an action that left the Nakayama family without a husband and father. Tosiwo became the man of the family and went to work. He earned enough money to take his mother and sisters back to Ulul, where his maternal relatives still lived. The young man remained with the family in Ulul until he was sure they would be all right. Then he announced that he wanted to go to school. He was sixteen, and until then he had never spent a day in a classroom.

Eventually Nakayama won a U.S. government scholarship and went to the University of Hawaii, where, as I wrote in my *Geographic* account, "the quality of his mind and personality attracted attention, and he was set on the track of leadership."

So it was that I resolved to go to Ulul and, as luck would have it, the *Micro Dawn* happened to have a week-long voyage to the island and its neighbors at a time I could go. An old hand in the islands and a new friend of mine, Sam McPhetres, archivist for the Trust Territory government, volunteered to go along and help us out if needed.

But during the planning stage Sam voiced a note of caution: "*All* field trips are late getting off, *all* take longer than expected, and there is no regular schedule." In other words, it would be risky.

By the time of the voyage I no longer had any illusions about the central Pacific being a "paradise," as many believe it to be. (All right, so I called it a paradise a couple of times in my *Geographic* story but only to focus attention on the contradictions such as "Pollution in Paradise," etc.) Apparently a forever-warm climate, palm trees, powder-soft sand beaches, clear blue water, and a continual parade of lovely clouds crossing an immense azure dome are enough to send the work-a-day world into a dream of ecstasy. But on the inhabited islands of the central Pacific the problems are serious and almost beyond solving.

Aside from beauty, natural resources are limited to coconut palms, a factor that severely hobbles the notion of a self-supporting, money making economy. Western-style education is new, unproved, and largely irrelevant for those who plan to stay home. Isolation makes the delivery of adequate medical care very difficult, and the traditions of the people coupled with the hot climate mitigate against change that might improve living conditions. The pace of life is slow: The extended family serves as a kind of social security, and the ambition to excel, to outshine others, is not regarded as a virtue.

Of course, most of the peoples of Micronesia have been living the traditional life for centuries. But now, with the intrusion of the twentieth century, the United States has taken its responsibilities in the area seriously, attempting to bring education and modern medicine to the islands. Radio transmitters have been installed so that each island can summon help in an emergency: Vital weather news provides an early-warning system against life-threatening hurricanes and typhoons. Peace Corps volunteers have been sent to teach sanitation, build latrines, and perform a hundred other tasks. And units from the U.S. armed forces have joined together in teams to build roads, bridges, schools, and hospitals on the larger islands.

Moreover, the U.S. vision of government responsibility has been picked up by the governments of the various new states and nations, as I would see the day we boarded the *Micro Dawn,* which, remarkably, was planning to sail only two days late. The cabin passengers included two teachers assigned to test students, a nutritionist checking on school lunch programs, a health officer concerned with the needs of the handicapped, and a young American physician, Dr. Don Preston, with a health aide, who would introduce prenatal care to pregnant women, inoculate their babies, and treat any maladies that might come his way.

We also met Father John Fahey, a Jesuit priest returning to his mission in the Western islands. A man in his early seventies,

Father Fahey was full of Irish wit and good humor. Standing at railside watching the *Micro Dawn* load, the priest broke the news that upon pulling anchor, the *Micro Dawn* would sail straight for the Westerns.

"But isn't the *Micro Dawn* going to Namonuito?" I inquired, startled at what looked like a change in what I had understood was the ship's schedule. The good father assured me that the ship was indeed scheduled to go to the atoll, but after the Westerns. As if to console, or perhaps prepare me, he added, "Out here we are constantly faced with either a crisis or an emergency. We are often chagrined but not surprised."

The scene at the dock in Moen, capital of Truk, may no longer have surprised Father Fahey, but it was full of the unusual and unexpected for the *National Geographic* team, which included photographer David Hiser, my old friend from the Tasmanian coverage. In addition to Sam McPhetres, we also had with us John Uruo, a municipal affairs officer for Truk State, who would act as our interpreter of island language and life.

On her last story for National Geographic, Carolyn goes native with Pacific island friends. Photo by David Hiser.

We watched from railside as truck after truck arrived with canned goods and food staples from the United States—canned fruit (in a land where bananas grow wild), evaporated milk, mixed vegetables, green beans, shortening, and huge bags of rice, flour, and sugar. Much of the food, Sam told me, would go to the school lunch program. Consumer goods, such as fabric for a skirt or *thu,* went into the ship's hold to be sold to islanders after they had earned the necessary cash from their copra, which would make the return voyage to Moen.

Throughout the day came the families who were returning to their homes on the islands via the *Micro Dawn*. They had been gone for months, many for years, since, Sam explained once again, the ships do not operate on a schedule and as long as four months may elapse between trips. The men wore their *thus,* brightly colored strips of cloth drawn tight between the legs and tied around the waist with loose ends dangling; the bare-breasted women dressed in grass skirts; the children were naked. They brought their own food—taro root cooked and wrapped in green leaves—and drink—bags of coconuts ready to be tapped for their refreshing milk. Some were taking home live chickens stuffed into straw bags. One family traveled with a caged pig that unmercifully squealed in terror throughout the voyage—and directly beneath my porthole as well.

As time to sail drew near, half of Moen, it seemed, came down to the dock to wave us off: area directors of the Peace Corps with packages for young people stationed on the islands; fellow priests bidding farewell to Father Fahey; and friends and relatives of the government teams, the deck passengers, and the ship's officers and crew. The poignancy of the farewells came as confirmation of the uncertainty of travel in the Far Pacific.

When the *Micro Dawn* weighed anchor about 4 P.M., we turned to explore the ship. As I had concluded earlier, most of the returning Western islanders would camp out on deck and little family groups were busily staking claims to their own bits of space. There were shipboard toilets for them but the kids didn't bother with such amenities. Standing at railside below top deck, I learned to watch out for small streams of urine coming from above.

We, along with the government teams, were cabin passengers, and, no doubt in deference to my age, nationality, and sex, I, with Pat of course, was assigned the so-called owner's cabin—the best passenger accommodation aboard. The owner's cabin could not be termed luxurious in any sense but it did have a private shower and toilet, the only such exclusive facility available. Shortly after inspecting the communal toilet facilities for cabin passengers, Sam and David let me know that they would happily accept an invitation to use our bathroom, and it was immediately extended.

We also had a large private refrigerator that, I suspect, had never been cleaned through decades of use, with the result that I had to hold my nose whenever I opened its door. I didn't feel up to the monumental scouring required so we used the refrigerator only for canned soft drinks.

At dinnertime we found our way, along with the other cabin-class passengers and ship's officers, to the dining room, the only public space except for the crowded decks. The room was small and jammed with a half dozen tables. Our fellow passengers were a somber lot who ate rapidly and without conversation. Dr. Don and Father Fahey joined the *Geographic* team at dinner, and I think we made enough talk and laughter to make up for the rest.

In the beginning the young purser did his best to please, but after a couple of days he disappeared and remained out of sight for the rest of the voyage. In the end we learned why. But I leap ahead of my story.

After dinner we strolled on the decks, threading family groups sprawled on straw mats and asleep at the first failing of light. The sea was silvery under starlight with phosphorescent highlights. The churning of the ship's engine was reassuring. We were starting a voyage to back-of-beyond. My heart leaped at the sheer adventure of it all.

The next morning we awoke to find the ship's motors stilled and the deckhands launching the two motorized deck boats that would transport all passengers desiring to go ashore to the island of Pulap.

We quickly dressed, ate breakfast, and lined up to board one of the boats bound for shore. As we waited, Sam strolled up to suggest we accompany him to the stern of the boat. "I thought you would like to see the sharks," he said, pointing to five huge creatures feeding on ship's garbage. "They must be following us about."

The presence of sharks in the immediate area was not reassuring when we discovered the procedure of boarding the motorized deck boats, now bobbing up and down in the swells far below the deck. Pat, who in certain situations tends to regard his seventy years as something of a hindrance, was struck by the dangers we were about to face. Each of us had to climb down the side of the ship on a rusty ladder affixed to the hull so closely that there was no room for toes to surely grip its rungs. At the end of the ladder, if one got that far without mishap, we had to leap for the boat several feet below. The distance of the leap depended on the swells in the sea, so timing of the leap was all-important. While the agile young seamen who operated the boats thought nothing of such action—and therefore did not think to offer us a helping hand—our inexperience coupled with a certain dread of being injured in this remote spot made us hesitant and fearful. Just about the time that Pat or I would get our courage up to make the leap, the boat had dropped to the bottom of a wave and the distance between us and the target had grown dangerously large.

Carolyn sits in the cockpit of a downed Japanese aircraft while diving on the Japanese fleet sunk during World War II. Photo by David Hiser.

Despite all, we finally managed to make the tender unscathed, thanks to the help of David Hiser, whose steady hand and strong arms were ever ready to help his creaking colleagues. Our boatman dropped us off at the rickety dock on Pulap Island.

The place looked like a tropical idyll: sandy pathways threading swaying palm trees, huts with walls and roofs of palm fronds, people dressed as our deck passengers in thus and grass skirts. Although only mid-morning, already the kitchen huts, actually small lean-tos walled only against the sea breezes, were enveloped in smoke as women bent to barbecue fatty turkey tails, an all-time delicacy of Truk islanders, according to Sam. The turkey tails had arrived aboard the *Micro Dawn* frozen and packed in huge boxes in such quantity that I suspected that the vast majority of turkey tails sold on earth go straight to the central Pacific.

While mothers cooked this favorite dish, the island's children quickly found their favorite person—Father Fahey—whom they followed around like he was the Pied Piper. Ringing a church bell, Father Fahey lost no time in calling all to Pulap's tiny white chapel. I will never forget the endearing sight of the island's children, seated on the dirt floor of the chapel, looking up at Father Fahey, their faces aglow with love and interest. They were, in fact, the liveliest people on Pulap.

As we walked about, we failed to find an offered hand of friendship, or even a smiling hello from the adults. The girls and women seemed afraid of us and would scurry by in a crouched position, their eyes downcast, when approaching any of the men in our party. But it wasn't just our party the women crouched before; it was all men—island custom, I was assured, and just a way the women had of showing deference to their elders (or to the male sex, I concluded privately). It was not the first time I had encountered how severely the cultures in the central Pacific degrade women. In Yap, another Federated State of Micronesia, for example, most women are not even allowed to eat from the same taro patch as the men, much less—heaven forbid—dine with their masters. Throughout my coverage in the Pacific, I was accorded something like an honorary male status. But while I asked all the questions and took all the notes, the men I interviewed invariably answered to Pat rather than me, whenever he happened to be present.

We found Pulap's older men sitting or sprawled about on straw mats in the Men's House, a large open-sided pavilion, drinking something from recycled bottles. Curiously, the men seemed to have little interest in us, although we were most certainly the only visitors, other than nearby islanders, to have called at Pulap in months. The men seemed dazed and we shortly learned why. When John Uruo organized a little welcome for us from a couple of the island's head men, we were offered a drink from the same kind of bottles the men were drinking from and discovered that they contained homemade coconut wine. It was a heady brew, as the condition of the men testified, and we felt disinclined to imbibe more than a sip, for politeness sake. After all, we had to leap for the ship's ladder when we returned aboard.

Throughout the day, the ship's tenders made trip after trip, bringing to the island the food for the school lunch program and taking to the ship copra and those island shoppers who could afford the *Micro Dawn*'s store of consumer goods. Meanwhile, the government teams went about their various jobs, testing students, dispensing medicine, organizing school lunch programs, and gathering information.

At dusk we, too, gathered on the shore to await the next tender. There, sprawled out on the sand, was our ship's captain, dead drunk. Pulap, it was explained, was the captain's home island. He hadn't been home for a long time: A celebration was understandable. I just hoped that the first mate could manage the ship's operation alone.

But we were not to sail anywhere for four days, although the copra was loaded and the shopping completed during the first day. As Sam pointed out, the government ships had no schedule. The captain of this one wanted a longer visit with his relatives and his wishes came first, before those of his deck passengers waiting to get to their own homes on other islands. The captain's wishes came before the government teams bent on service to other communities and before our hope to visit the Ulul relatives of so notable a personage as the nation's president. Stuck, we made use of our time as best we could, daily risking our necks climbing down the hazardous ship's ladder to jump for the motorboat that would take us to shore and reversing the action each evening on returning to the ship.

We sailed for tiny Tamatam, 15 minutes away and within sight of Pulap, and stayed for another two days. The routine there was the same but on so small an island the copra was loaded in a couple of hours. We had virtually shot a week on only two islands, and there were two much larger islands in the Westerns that we were to visit before turning north to Ulul. I gave up hope, at that stage, of ever completing the voyage we had planned, so we radioed Moen to send a chartered boat to pick us up at Puluwat, our next stop, an overnight sail from Tamatam.

Unlike Pulap and Tamatam, the island of Puluwat wears a near-to-shore ring of coral, with an opening to the sea too shallow and narrow for the *Micro Dawn* to pass through. As a consequence, we had to anchor in the open sea, a circumstance that tripled the danger of getting off and on the ship since the waves were monumental and the small tenders rose higher and fell deeper with each swell. Make no mistake—we were frightened but there was no other way to get ashore if we wished to visit Puluwat.

"From the sea," began my *Geographic* story on the new nations in the Pacific, "Puluwat is every man's dream of a paradise: an island set in the blue depths of the Pacific, ringed by a coral reef that encloses a crystal clear lagoon. Ashore it looks like a garden, with towering coconut palms lining the broad sandy paths and great old breadfruit trees, their roots clutching the earth like gnarled fists, rising majestically above the green banana and taro patches."

Some eighteen years earlier, John Uruo, Truk's municipal affairs officer who was our companion and guide on the voyage, had left his home on Puluwat to go to college in the United States. During the feast, which was held in his honor before leaving, John stood to speak his mind. "I go to jump over the wall," he said. The wall John sought to leap was one of isolation, poor health care and education, and meager financial resources. I wondered how much of that wall had fallen in Puluwat, a larger, more important place than Pulap or Tamatam, since John had left.

Well, the Peace Corps was there, which, from my perspective, reduced the isolation. Eric Sanford, the volunteer on duty during my visit, had devoted a good part of his tour to improving sanitary conditions and teaching good hygiene. He told me that, following the 1982 cholera epidemic that broke out in Truk, he helped install sixty latrines.

"I spoke to each family," he said, "emphasizing the importance of toilets to everyone's health. Yet today only about 10 percent of the islanders use them." On the success side, Eric also helped build twenty-nine water catchment tanks that were most welcome since they provide healthier drinking water as well as plenty of water for the showers that the people love to take. Another success, achieved by the islanders themselves, was the Puluwat Middle School. While the government supported an elementary school, students in junior and senior high school formerly had to sail to distant Ulul—on one of those irregular government ships—where they would remain for months or years separated from their families. With the Puluwat Middle School, a beautiful complex of thatched-roofed huts built by the parents, the younger kids could now stay home to study. Their teachers were islanders who had been educated in colleges and universities in the United States and who had returned home to help their people.

It was my pleasure to listen in as the government-sent educators tested Puluwat's students and consulted with their teachers. The bright kids would be encouraged to go on to the high school in Ulul and, ultimately, to college in the United States.

I also visited Dr. Don, who oversaw the inoculation of babies by the island's resident health aide in his small clinic. The physician spent most of his time teaching the health aides on his beat so that they might themselves accomplish simple procedures, such as inoculations, and learn to recognize life-threatening illnesses that would warrant notifying the authorities in Moen.

With his mission headquartered in Puluwat, Father Fahey held a continual round of religious services and educational programs in a large church built by his devout congregation. I wondered how one man—not too young at that—could run so hard throughout the day. He wouldn't have such a killer schedule in a U.S. city. I invited myself to visit his home, a thatch-roofed hut near the church, but the priest smilingly declined to receive me saying, "I am a bachelor, and you know how we are. We don't keep things so neat in the house."

For the Puluwat visit, we moved ashore and lived in a kind of guest house near the school, an arrangement that spared us the dangerous daily off-and-on boarding of the *Micro Dawn*. John arranged for island friends to bring in meals and we feasted on fresh crab and fish, barbecued pork, breadfruit salad (not unlike potato salad but better), and just-picked bananas.

John also got me a ride aboard an outrigger canoe. The Pacific islanders are world-class sailors, having crossed vast distances in their dugout canoes with unerring accuracy by reading cloud formations, directions of currents, flights of birds, and positions of the sun, moon, and stars to guide them. Once the canoe took sailors on voyages between islands but now it was used mostly to carry lighter cargo from the freighters, to fish the nearby waters, and for pleasure.

While I enjoyed the novelty of my sail with the Puluwat men, I can attest to the fact that the outrigger canoe is not very comfortable. That is because there is so little of it to hang on to. The master of the vessel assigns what passes for seats in order to achieve a balance. My "seat" was over the water on the outrigger structure itself. Every time we changed direction and the boom came about, I had to duck or else be knocked overboard by the boom. Since we changed direction constantly, I was in a continual state of bowing deeply, while clinging to my perch for dear life. Each bow brought me eyeball-to-eyeball with water and waves since the canoe sits low in the sea. Some, if not most, bows left me drenched, which was no big deal since it was warm and sunny, but it was hard, if not risky, to breathe with water splashing in my face.

My fellow sailors appeared to be completely unaffected. But, of course, they stood up much of the time, defying gravity. Standing up is a feat those with no experience attempt at their peril. I marveled again that the ancestors of these people lived aboard such canoes for weeks, perhaps even months, sailing on and on and on, ever facing the perils of the sea. Such endurance, such courage!

As a matter of fact, the same endurance and courage was exhibited by a group of Puluwat sailors only a few years ago. I met an old Puluwat chief who told me his sad story.

Some men, he didn't know who, came to Puluwat in 1975 and invited him and Puluwat's sailors to bring their outrigger canoe to New York and parade with the tall ships in honor of the bicentennial of the United States. If the chief and his crew would sail to Saipan in the Northern Marianas, it was promised, they and the canoe would be picked up and flown to New York. When the islanders got to Saipan—a two-week, night-and-day sail—they waited and waited for word from those who had invited them to the bicentennial. But no word came and they had no way to get to New York on their own. Eventually the men left their canoe in Saipan, where I saw it on display in the Saipan airport, and returned home by air.

The old wound still rankled, I could see, and so I crawled out on a limb and made a daring proposal. Perhaps the *National Geographic* magazine would be willing to sponsor the Puluwat crew for a sail in the upcoming Statue of Liberty Tall Ships Parade. The old man was all smiles as I told him good-bye. But this part of the story did not have a happy ending either.

After three days on Puluwat, the boat we had chartered from Moen by radio finally turned up. The boat, called *Miss Namonuito,* was late because it had gotten lost, the twenty-six-year-old, first-time-out captain explained. Moreover, the radio only worked when the boat's motor was turned off. Looking down from the deck of the *Micro Dawn* at the motley crew of young men and listening to the kid in command, I came to the decision that it might be better to take our chances with the *Micro Dawn* even if it took much longer.

And lucky we did. After returning to Washington I got a report from a Moen friend: "I thought you'd like to hear what you missed by not taking the *Miss Namonuito* back to Moen. Once more the crew got lost and this time wound up in Ulul. Then they set out from Ulul and got lost again. At last radio report the captain was going to give up sailing. When we stopped by Ulul this trip to drop off the high school students, there was the *Miss Namonuito,* resigned to exile."

But the *Micro Dawn,* itself, was increasingly a chancy proposition. Returning to it on the last evening at Puluwat, the boat operator and several of the ship's crew were all heavily drinking coconut wine. Passing the bottle around, our companions showed their displeasure at our refusal to join them in a drink. At shipside, the boat operator, now drunk, made little effort to bring his vessel near the ladder. Once again, David Hiser took command, maneuvered the boat nearer to the ship and fairly pulled Pat and me onto the ladder and up to the deck. By this time most of the ship's crew, including the long-missing ship's purser, appeared to be passed out from the coconut wine.

When we arrived at Pulusuk the next morning, I decided not to go ashore, preferring to leave that Western island to a dream of beauty, looking from the distance like the paradise it could never be.

After Pulusuk the *Micro Dawn* limped back to Truk, with scant food and water, one motor out, and the radar on the blink. Upon sighting land, I felt profound relief to have made a safe return to an island linked to the outside world by regular air service. And I gave up any thought about being a perfect traveler since, despite Kazantzakis, no one could have created the country where I had just traveled, except the people who lived there.

Back in Washington, I set to work on arrangements to bring the Puluwat sailors to New York for the Tall Ship Parade at the rededication of the Statue of Liberty. The National Geographic Society immediately agreed to sponsor the sailors' visit and Air Micronesia and Continental Air promised free transportation for the men. I got the U.S. Army to agree to land a cargo plane at Moen, pick up the canoe, and deliver it to the New York vicinity. I spoke to a friend in the White House who promised that President Ronald Reagan, in reviewing the Tall Ship Parade, would recognize the Pacific sailors as coming from a new nation that the United States helped bring into being. I went to New York and reserved rooms at an apartment hotel where the islanders might cook their own meals. Further, I planned that after the Tall Ship Parade the outrigger canoe would go on display in Rockefeller Center with the sailors, in native dress or undress, standing guard during the day. I even arranged for a security guard to watch over the canoe by night.

I left until last one tiny little detail: to get the New York Yacht Club, which was in charge of the parade, to issue an invitation to the Pacific sailors. Then came the shocker. The club refused!

"But why?" I cried.

"Because we can't have grown men urinating in public, since there is no head (read toilet) on an outrigger canoe."

"No worry there," I replied, "because I'll hire a motorboat that does have a toilet on board and every time one of the sailors has to go, he can run up a little flag and we can bring the motorboat alongside for the sailor's use."

But the answer was still an emphatic "No."

There was nothing I could do, except conclude that members of the New York Yacht Club could not abide to have men of color outsailing them.

CHAPTER 14

Adventure in the Ages ...
and in Different Voices

Behold my covenant is with thee and
thou shalt be a father of many nations.

—*Genesis 17:4*

ROWING UP IN MISSISSIPPI IN THE 1930s, I knew that the Jewish people were in terrible danger in a Europe where the Nazis were in the ascendancy. *Time* magazine detailed Kristallnacht (Night of Broken Glass), November 9, 1938, in all its horror. The handwriting was clearly on the wall for everyone to see. From that time on I yearned for the United States to go to war to save the Jewish people. After Germany invaded Poland in 1939 and Great Britain declared war, I was even more anxious. But what can an eighteen-year-old southern girl do to influence world events? Nothing much, of course, but in my own way I could try to make it up to the Jewish people.

I could marry a Jewish boy, for example. Alas, there were only a handful of Jewish people living in Kosciusko, and the only eligible lad about my age had already fallen in love with my cousin, Nancy Love Comfort, and she with him. In college I dated every Jewish boy who invited me out, especially at the University of Missouri, where the Chi Omega house where I lived had a rule against dating Jews. The only thing I held against Pat, the man I married, was that he had no known Jewish ancestral connection.

No matter, I still yearned to do my bit to make up to the Jewish people for the Holocaust. And my chance came with the

National Geographic magazine. We had covered the Egyptians, the Greeks, the Romans, the Etruscans, the Celts, the Vikings, and many other peoples of distinctive cultures. Why not do a story on the Jewish people? I went to then-editor Gil Grosvenor with the idea. And he was receptive.

"But Carolyn, you are going to have to have a special angle for the story. It won't do just to write a history of the Jews. Whole libraries have been devoted to the subject. Come up with ideas of how you might cover the Jews and submit it to me. Then, we'll see."

And to help me find my angle, Gil sent me to study at the Museum of the Diaspora in Tel Aviv, Israel. About the same time, a representative of Israeli Tourism in New York, Geoffrey Weill, a man of great charm and a personal friend, invited Pat and me to come to Israel on a press tour. It was my first visit to Israel and Geoffrey saw to it that it was perfect. He read the Sermon on the Mount where Christ preached it. He took us to the Western ("Wailing") Wall in Jerusalem where Pat was invited to pray with Jewish men. We visited Bethlehem and worshipped with Christians. We recognized the sanctity of the Dome of the Rock, built on the site of the Jewish Temple destroyed by the Romans, to those of Moslem faith. And Geoffrey introduced us to his brother Asher, thirteen years his senior, who was an Israeli citizen and editor of *Ariel,* Israel's leading cultural magazine.

After studying at the Museum of the Diaspora, I thought I had the idea that would make the story for the *National Geographic.* We should try to find a family that, in itself, represented the scattering of the Jewish people—the Diaspora—since the destruction of the Second Temple in A.D. 70. Dining with Geoffrey and Asher near the end of my stay in Israel, I told them of my idea. And in that instant, a miracle happened. I discovered that the

Carolyn in London with the Weill brothers, Asher (left) and Geoffrey. Photo by Nathan Benn.

Weill brothers, their parents, and their ancestors were just the family I was looking for. Their father, born in London, was an Ashkenazi, a branch of European Jewry, and he traced his family, generation by generation, back to the fourteenth century. Kurt Weill, the composer, was a member of the family. The mother was a Sephardi, the other ranking branch of Jewry, and traced her family, through tradition, back to the second century A.D.—and perhaps earlier. Geoffrey had emigrated to New York City, the city with the largest population of Jews in the world; Asher had emigrated to Israel and lived in Jerusalem, the holy city of the Jewish people.

Would the Weill family be willing to hit the road with a *National Geographic* team and visit all the sites where the family had been known to have lived to develop a kind of Jewish "Roots" story? Yes, yes, yes, came my answer.

Back in Washington I sold the whole concept to Gil Grosvenor, who gave me a hefty travel budget and unlimited time for the coverage. But there was one stipulation: Although I would write the story, the Weill brothers would be asked to sign it. Gil felt it was more appropriate for the authors to be Jewish as well as the photographer. So we had the marvelous talent of Nathan Benn to enhance the images of this immense journey.

Although both Geoffrey and Asher are fine writers in their own right, they graciously agreed to let me write the story that they would sign since, they felt, I most surely had more experience writing for the *National Geographic* than did they. The story we spun—the Weill family, Nathan, and I—was covered, written, and photographed. But it never ran in the magazine. By the time it was completed, Gil, who had assigned me the story, was no longer editor. The story was given to the brothers Weill to use in any way they saw fit, and they gave it to me for publication in this book. Although I have kept the story in their voices, I was witness to every action, every emotion. The Jewish Diaspora story was the crowning achievement of my life with *National Geographic,* and the Weill brothers and I give it to you with our blessing.

I

Asher Speaks

In the renewal of a spring-fresh day last June, we start on the road back—back to our youth, back through the lives of our parents, grandparents, and successive generations of ancestors, back through time itself, the only homeland that our people had known through centuries of wandering.

We are Jews, my brother Geoffrey and I, but we are also British, born and educated in England. I am an Israeli as well, while Geoffrey is a citizen of the United States, joining the six million who compose the largest Jewish community on earth.

We sit in the spacious, high-ceilinged London flat of our parents, fingering old family portraits and talking. Through the tall windows we glimpse through the trees the green dome of the Spanish and Portuguese Synagogue, of which our Moroccan-born great-grandfather was a founding member.

His granddaughter, our mother, is Violet Afriat Weill and belongs to that branch of Jewry known as Sephardi. She traces one branch of her ancestry directly to the Golden Age of the Jews in Spain.

Our father, Bernard Max Weill, counts as second of the two branches of Jewry known as Ashkenazi. His ancestors, hailing from the Black Forest region of Germany, are documented generation by generation as far back as 1381 to Rabbi Jacob ben Judah Weil, whose wife's claimed descent is from a giant intellect of medieval times, Rabbi Meir of Rothenburg.

Our mother's blonde hair and peach complexion recalls yet another heritage, that of her Scottish Unitarian mother, Kate May Campbell of Melbourne, Australia. It was at that same Spanish and Portuguese Synagogue that Kate was converted to Judaism by the Sephardi Chief Rabbi of the British Empire.

And so, counting only three generations, our family is quite an international and ecumenical mix with strains of Scottish, Australian, Moroccan, English and German, Israeli and American, with Hebrew, Christian, and probably agnostic beliefs all mixed. What we share, however, is the crowning realization of being Jews.

For me it was not always so. I was a child of World War II and moved to the countryside during the bombing of London. Shortly after the war, I went to a Church of England boarding school. With my father in the British army and my mother working, I had no religious education and little sense of being Jewish until I was twelve years old, with my Bar Mitzvah imminent and the family reunited in London. Enrolled in the City of London School—at the time the only great English private school with no Jewish quota—I found my happiest days as a champion swimmer, an army cadet sergeant, and one of the prefects who helped the staff run the school.

Born after the war, thirteen years my junior, Geoffrey went to Hebrew School at the Spanish and Portuguese Synagogue and followed me to the City of London School but not to the fulfillment that I found there. He was always—unlike me—conscious of his Jewishness and easily perceived dislike, discrimination, even anti-Semitism.

Nevertheless, really for my sake, we are off for a visit to the school. We drive along the Thames and pause before the school's monumental granite columns, iron grilles, and enormous oak portals, as proud a building as any along that proud river. And pride is what I feel upon seeing again the school that shaped my youth.

In the entrance hall, we stop to read the marble plaques. One explains that the school was founded near St. Paul's Cathedral in 1472 and moved Thames-side in December 1882, when the Prince of Wales dedicated the building.

Another plaque tells that Lionel Rothschild—Lord Rothschild—the first Jewish peer and an international financier, disbursed scholarships to commemorate his acceptance as the first Jew in Parliament. That acceptance was sponsored by Benjamin Disraeli, a Jewish convert to Christianity who founded the Conservative Party and became prime minister to her majesty Queen Victoria.

Before leaving the school I visit for one last time my special haunt, the swimming pool where I once swam 200 laps a day. Then I drop by the lavatories. There, freshly scrawled, are the words, "Jews burn easily."

The Narrator Speaks

"Jews burn easily!" The history of the Jews often seems but a variation on the theme. Tel Aviv's Beit Hatefutsoth, the Museum of the Jewish Diaspora, displays fifty-two Scrolls of Fire, one for each week of the year, and each tells a horrendous tale.

Destruction of the Temple, A.D. 70: "All night seas of flame raged about the Temple Mount ... the Romans could shout in triumph over a city defiled in its own blood, filled with people starved to death and slaughtered by the sword, embers, and heaps of ashes."

The First Crusade, 1096: "From Rouen in Normandy ... to Jerusalem, they murdered the Jews. And in the communities of the Rhine eleven hundred were sacrificed in one day."

Years of the Black Plague, 1348–1352: "My son, do not say ... that it was only a people caught up in madness who heaped tens of thousands of Jews, old men and babies, men and women, on bonfires in three hundred cities in Europe .... A black hatred of Israel preceded the plague."

Massacre of Jews by the Cossacks, Poles, Russians, and Swedes, 1648–1666: "The Cossacks stripped off their skin and threw their severed limbs to the dogs. Children were killed at their mothers' breasts, or roasted alive on spits over the fire."

Pogroms of South Russia, 1881–1883: "Huge mobs attacked our houses with overwhelming fury. They got drunk before nightfall. Priests blessed them as they set out. The slogan—'Beat the Jews and Save Russia.'"

Such horrifying episodes actually only punctuate Jewish history. The real lines of that history reveal triumph after triumph in the face of overwhelming odds, against all possibility of success, to win survival over and after thousands of years.

II
Geoffrey Speaks

They gathered that Thursday, as every Thursday for as long as anyone could remember, for morning worship in their small synagogue, passing through iron gates beneath the Hebrew legend, "This is nothing else but the house of God."

The Jews of Kippenheim, Germany, along with Jews throughout Germany, would remember well the date November 9, 1938: Kristallnacht, Hitler's first mass attack, arrest, and detention of Jewish citizens.

As the service ended and the congregation filed out, uniformed SS troops seized the Jewish men, arrested them, and marched them off to the jail in the Rathaus, or City Hall. Then, returning to the synagogue, the Nazis ransacked, looted, and set it afire.

Forty-one years later, we step through the same iron gates and enter the ravished house of prayer. Bare of furnishing, it is now a storehouse for a farmer's cooperative. Windows are boarded; plaster, once painted to beautify a sanctuary, litters the floor. A pin-up photograph of a half-nude woman desecrates the spot where the Ark had stood, holding the Scrolls of the Law.

Asher joins me and together we begin to whisper the Kaddish, the Hebrew prayer for the dead: "Magnified and sanctified be His great name in the world which He has created according to His will."

We pray for the warm and vibrant Jewish life that once flourished in Kippenheim, for a host of cousins and ancestors who made this town their home. The first of the family to come was Rabbi Eliezer Lazarus Weyl (Weill), who moved here from Stuehlingen on the Swiss-German border in the early 1700s.

My brother and I have returned with our parents and wives to discover what remains of our roots in a village where Jew and Christian once lived in prosperity and friendship.

We sit in the sunshine beside the town fountain on the main street, and, sipping a cold beer, Pa remembers how it was. In 1899 his father, Simon Weill, was bitten by wanderlust at the age of eighteen and left for London, where he did well as the representative of German manufacturers.

"My sister, Esme, and I spent most of our summers here, playing with our cousins and being spoiled by our grandparents," Pa recalls.

"In those days—the 1920s—Kippenheim's Christians would drop in on Jewish families to help them celebrate the Holy Days, and the town's fifty-odd Jewish families would return the visits at Christmas or Easter."

Pa points to a shop down the street: "That was cousin Herman Wertheimer's hardware store and his home next door. Herman's son Henry and the other Kippenheim men arrested by the SS on Kristallnacht were sent to the concentration camp at Dachau. When my father learned of it, he went to the British Home Office in London and swore out affidavits of support for about twenty of our cousins and friends, making it possible for them to escape to safety in England."

A pretty little town in the Black Forest, Kippenheim, with steep-roofed houses painted green, orange, brown, and gray, with shutters of contrasting colors, with flowers in window boxes, with about 3,000 people—none of them Jews.

We walk a block to the home where our grandfather was born and its present owner allows us inside to look about. With family pictures in hand we identify the rooms, pausing in the bedroom of Great Uncle Fritz and Great Aunt Claire, who slit her throat while sitting before her dressing table mirror a few months before Kristallnacht. A widow, her only son had fled a darkening Germany.

Does anyone remember Fritz and Claire and the rest of the family? Yes, say the Dorners, two elderly people who live near the Wertheimer house. They get out their boxes of pictures and pore over them with Pa, groping back through the years. A face here, a name there. Just scraps of memory.

Finally, we drop in on the town historian, an old man with bald head and watery blue eyes, who tells us that a book is being written about Kippenheim, with thirty-one entries on Weills, and that Kippenheimers still use all sorts of Jewish words and still call a restaurant "Herschele," an affectionate name for its former Jewish owner.

But, ironically, he claims not to know how the last Jews left town, or what happened in Kippenheim on Kristallnacht. Nor did he know Claire.

We stand beside Claire's grave amid the venerable cedars of the Jewish cemetery, miraculously still intact, on a hillside in the nearby hamlet of Schmieheim, and ponder the torment of her last days. Stepping among the tall-standing terra-cotta gravestones, we pass as in review of an army and salute this testimony to the hundreds who lived out their lives in a beautiful and fruitful land.

We find the grave of our father's mother, who died when he was eighteen, and read the inscription on her tombstone: "Of this wide world, the loveliest and best, has smiled, said goodnight, and gone to rest."

And amid the birdsong and the gentle surf of wind in cedar, we are struck by the enormity of death. Yet, somehow, at this place, it is more. Here and there, tombstones set to mark the double grave of a married couple show interment of only one mate; the missing one, as words chiseled in stone after World War II reveal "Deported to Poland" or "Victim of Holocaust."

We huddle together in desolation.

III
Asher Speaks

It is cold, as the desert often is after night falls, with only the bare bones of rock to stop the wind ravaging across empty spaces. Our small party, including my two sons, fifteen-year-old Ilan and eleven-year-old Ayal, draws close beneath the wall of Saint Catherine's Monastery, shelter for Greek Orthodox monks since the sixth century. The camels are late so we must wait to start our ascent of Mount Sinai, revered by Jew, Christian, and Moslem as the place where, by tradition, God gave the world the Ten Commandments.

Arava, our guide, explains: "The Bedouin need the light of the moon before risking the camels on the rough trail. They will come."

But it is nearly ten o'clock, with the temperature near freezing, before the moon shoulders over a mountain to flood with spectral light the canyon that is our way to the top. The camels come, we mount, and move off.

It is slow going and steep and the camels groan with the effort. For 2 hours we climb, switching back and forth, first in canyons, then on the flank of the mountain. Finally, rounding a bend, I look up to a sight that clutches the heart with awe. Mount Sinai's peak rises before us, sheer and incredibly high, a ghostly mass of enormity, leaping into infinity itself.

Now we must dismount and clamber up a rocky trail for another half an hour, to the foot of the escarpment. There, flat-sided boulders, piled on top of one another, wind upward—two thousand steps, placed there as his life's work by a single monk from Saint Catherine's, it is said.

We climb, muscles straining, lungs aching, buffeted by wind and with nothing above us but a setting moon and a silent host of stars. And finally we achieve the summit where we plan to meet the dawn in prayer.

The sun comes, piercing the blue of the heavenly dome and bathing us in a golden glow, as my sons and I sit on red rocks and see for the first time a granite scape of barren mountains, so lofty, so far-reaching, so forever as to seem a manifestation of God himself. It is the wilderness of Sinai where God promised the Jews, "If you will obey my voice and keep my covenant, you shall be my own possession among all people."

I read aloud from the Psalms: "The Lord reigns; let the earth rejoice ... the mountains melt like wax before the Lord." And

Ilan reads aloud: "O sing to the Lord a new song, for he has done marvelous things."

I, too, pray: "Do Thou spread the tabernacle of Thy peace upon all the dwellers on earth." In this place so eloquent with God's majesty and power, I ache for my prayer to be heard and granted for Israelis, like ourselves, and for all people, everywhere.

Looking at my young sons, who must face, as all human beings, the constant threat of tragedy, I am astonished at the gallantry of humankind in finding meaning, love, and laughter amid life's mysteries. It is one of the great miracles and it is all clear to me on the mountain known as Sinai, where my ancestors and those of all Jews found their identity on the way to the Promised Land.

Now, to our reborn Promised Land, no bigger than the state of New Jersey, the Jews have poured: the pitiful remnant of European Jewry after the Holocaust, the North Africans and Eastern Europeans made unwelcome in lands they had inhabited for centuries by the thirty years of hostility between Israel and its Arab neighbors, Soviet Jews driven to emigrate—if allowed—by increasing pressures, and those like myself who simply regard Israel as home.

Various members of our family have, of course, come to Israel. One of the earliest, that we know about, was my father's first cousin, Leo or Arieh (both mean "lion") Weill, who fled Freiburg, Germany, as a young man of twenty-two in the year 1937 to come to what was then Palestine, a British-mandated territory.

He settled at Kibbutz Tirat Zvi, a religious community in the Jordan Valley. He fell in love with a young woman, Rivka, who was born in Latvia. For a time, Arieh's Promised Land looked promising indeed.

On the trail of our family roots, Ayal, my seven-year-old daughter Orit, and I drive to Tirat Zvi, in the Jordan Valley, where green lawns, palm trees, and pink and white oleanders surround neat bungalows. There is little to remind us of the frantic birth of the place or the danger that clouded much of its life.

But the Arabs fought against the settlement's survival. For two months, early in 1939, Tirat Zvi was cut off, beleaguered by enemy forces. Then, desperate for supplies, five men, including Arieh Weill, slipped out and made it to a nearby kibbutz. On their return, Arab gunfire cut down Arieh and a comrade.

We stand on the hill where our cousin died. The dirt path he used is paved now and lined with tall casuarina trees. A bus stop is near to where he fell. Cleared fields, freshly harrowed and ready for the planting of cotton, carrots, and alfalfa, open a broad and beautiful view to the River Jordan and beyond, to barren hills and a green plateau in the Hashemite Kingdom of Jordan.

At the kibbutz, we meet with its archivist, Ephraim Yair, who introduces us to Rivka Dolev—yes, the same Rivka that Arieh loved but now long married and a grandmother.

With astonishment we and the archivist learn that Rivka has saved, for over forty years, the few poignant possessions of her young friend: address book, family trees, diaries, prayer book, bankbook, a photograph album, which I open to a picture of my grandfather, and perhaps, most moving of all, a check for one guinea sent by my grandfather in London, which Arieh had not yet managed to deposit. The single letter received at the kibbutz after Arieh died: a sad little note from his mother, Ida Marx Weill, writing from Gurs, the Vichy French concentration camp in the Pyrenees, to which she had been deported from Germany in October 1940. She thanked the kibbutz for having buried her son. But Arieh's keepsakes never went to his mother because she, too, died—in a gas chamber at Auschwitz.

Since we are the first relatives to show interest in Arieh's fate, Rivka wants us to have his things, saying, "Today I feel as if the Day of Redemption has arrived."

We are deeply moved and briefly consider the kibbutz archives as the possible final repository of much of the memorabilia—after all, the young lion gave his life for this place and its way of life. In the end, however, I feel compelled to keep them in my sole possession.

IV
The Narrator Speaks

The flames of the burning temple in A.D. 70 signaled the beginning of the end of the Hebrew landhold in Palestine. Two wars and sixty-five years later, Rome cleared Jerusalem and Judea of all but a handful of Jews, ending a thousand years of Jewish sovereignty in the Promised Land.

Yet a blessing preceded the blow. A philosopher-rabbi, Yohanan ben Zakkai, living in the besieged Jerusalem, had himself smuggled out in a coffin to the tent of the Roman commander, Vespasian.

When the rabbi stepped out of the coffin he greeted the Roman with a prediction: Vespasian would be emperor. The favor: to allow the rabbi and his disciples to establish a school for the study of Jewish scripture. It was granted.

Thus was born, in nearby Yavneh, the first yeshiva, assuring thenceforth the power and influence of the rabbi—the Jewish intellectual. Thereafter, rabbis became, in fact, the rulers of the nation in Diaspora, directing universal Jewish literacy, purifying and preserving the Hebrew language, standardizing the religious liturgy, setting moral and spiritual standards, and establishing the machinery for self-government among far-flung communities, some as distant as India and China.

For centuries the Jews, through widely circulated commentaries called Responsa, explored for themselves new frontiers of social and spiritual progress. Some of the Responsa written by the fourteenth-century Weill patriarch Rabbi Jacob Weil are quoted to this day.

Meanwhile, Christianity and Islam gathered their adherents and, with temporal power ultimately secured, divided most of the world between them.

Almost from the beginning, and with only a few exceptions over the next millennium, Judaism and Islam dwelt in peace and mutual respect. Under Islam's benign eye, Jews attained brilliance in medicine, mathematics, architecture, philosophy, linguistics, astronomy, and diplomacy.

But they also remained pre-eminent in the crafts and in commerce, especially in trade across the vast North African and near eastern reaches of the Golden Crescent.

Geoffrey Speaks

We stand at the edge of the oasis, in the thrall of a drama of brilliant color. Striated and barren, red hills rise stark against a blue sky tufted with white clouds. Green young wheat grows in irrigated patches, spiky with date palm trees. The almond trees are pale puffs of blossoms; the olive trees, silvery, shimmering.

Never has earth seemed so life-giving, so forever spring, as in this place where my ancestors had lived for thousands of years. My mother, Violet Afriat Weill, and I had come home to Oufran or, as it is known today Ifrane de L'Anti-Atlas, in the southern desert of Morocco.

With family tradition our teacher we had heard that Jews of the Tribe of Ephraim settled here before Nebuchadnezzar destroyed Jerusalem's First Temple in 586 B.C. They established a Jewish kingdom, sometimes called the "Little" or "Second" Jerusalem, and the kingdom was ruled from Oufran by the Efrati (from Ephraim) family, whose name became Afriat.

Set astride the trans-Sahara trade route, a caravan stop between Timbuktu and Atlantic seaports, Oufran rose to importance, its Jews serving as the mainstay of commerce. Here, in the year 1846, my great-grandfather Aaron Afriat was born to a family wealthy from the trans-Sahara trade.

My great-grandfather left Oufran as a young man, moving with his family to Mogador, now Essaouira, where he helped build a prosperous business, trading in spices, gum, tea, and textiles. He went on to Tangier and married the beautiful Rahma Toledano, then finally on to London to establish the largest Anglo-Moroccan trading company of its day.

My mother remembers him: "Very successful, very elegant. He wore his silk top hat and morning suit to synagogue every Sabbath. My grandmother bought all her clothes in Paris. They would summer in Biarritz and winter in Monte Carlo. As a little girl, I was dazzled."

Threading the fields of Oufran and exploring the rough tracks of this birthplace of the London sophisticate, we see little that could dazzle and no suggestion of elegance. Missing, too, are Oufran's Jews, who have not lived here since the Israelis won the Six Day War in 1967 and stirred resentment against Jews everywhere in the near East.

Berber women in black robes till the fields and remind me of Ruth and Naomi in the Bible. Old men sit before mud houses, warming themselves in the sun and sipping green tea that was once known as "Afriat Tea," after its importer. A party of younger men fills the afternoon with jest and laughter while clearing an irrigation ditch. It could be 1,000 or 3,000 years ago.

We look for our ancestral home and find only a dubious site, the ruin of a large old house with arched windows and pale blue walls. We visit the synagogue, a small, bare, mud-plastered room maintained by Casablanca Jews. Perhaps my great-grandfather celebrated his Bar Mitzvah here. I light two candles to the dead.

The dead. Ah, yes. The cemetery remains. A desolate place on a barren hillside with rough-cut gravestones bearing Hebrew characters, now broken. Walls stand around the tomb of a revered rabbi, Joseph Ben Mimoun, believed to have died in 5 B.C. But nothing marks the remains of Eli "The Galilean," who was said to have brought Oufran the news of the destruction of the Second Temple.

Nothing speaks of our earliest known ancestors, Naftali and Yehuda Afriat, buried in this cemetery in A.D. 750 and 839, respectively.

And only the wind, keening amidst the barren hills, seems alive to bear witness to the mass burial here of the Nisrafim—the burned ones—fifty Jews who in 1792 chose suicide over forced conversion to Islam. The story unfolds, and, in the mind's eye, I see it all.

The soldiers of the Moslem ruler, BouHallais, build a huge pyre in the square of the village. Our ancestor, Rabbi Judah Ben Naftali Afriat, comforts each of the fifty, encouraging each to jump into the fire. Although suicide was forbidden, this action was to "sanctify god" ("Kiddush Hashem").

Last of all, Judah Afriat tears a gold earring from his ear, gives it to an onlooker for water to purify himself, and leaps into the flames, crying "Hear O Israel! The Lord Our God! The Lord Is One!"

Throughout my great-grandfather's life, my mother remembers, his pierced ear recalled the tragedy, and the whole Afriat clan still refrains from lighting fires on the anniversary of the martyrdom.

With the agonized bray of a donkey, we leave the cemetery and its horror to the dead. It is the living amongst our kin that now we seek.

Jewish life barely flickers at Mogador, a blue-and-white town with crenallated red walls overlooking a rock-splintered sea. A fragile remnant of thirty-nine adults, most of them elderly, are all who remain of the Jewish community of some twelve thousand in 1950. Nevertheless, we find cousins hitherto unknown to us, as we are unknown to them: Nathan Levy Ben-Sousan, the community president, and Isaac Afriat.

News of our visit had preceded us and we are invited, along with our cousins, to call upon the governor of Essaouira Province, His Excellency Abdallah Ouazzani, at his new blue-tiled palace on the outskirts of town.

Young, smiling, with dark hair and dark eyes, the governor offers us glasses of steaming mint tea and an equally refreshing portion of his views. He believes that it is tragic that so many Jews have emigrated from Morocco because his nation needs their expertise and training in economic affairs.

"If it were not for folly in the world," he says regretfully, "Arab wealth and Jewish genius could be partners to make a better life for all."

We are doubly welcomed by Mogador's Jewish community since it is so small that it can rarely raise a minyan, the ten adult men required for a prayer quorum, and our small party happily includes three Jewish males. It is Friday evening and the Sabbath can now begin with full worship service for the first time in months.

We gather in the small synagogue, beautiful with antique silver hanging lamps and carved mahogany furniture from England, and, in an especially graceful gesture, my mother and wife are seated in the sanctuary opposite the men, rather than in the separate room normally reserved for women. The age-old Hebrew rites begin, the same the world over, as easy for me to follow as a service in my own synagogue in New York. "Blessed art thou, oh Lord our God ... in love and favour hast given us thy holy Sabbath as an inheritance, a memorial of the creation."

At Isaac Afriat's home, we partake of the Sabbath feast, beginning with the familiar ritual. Isaac pours wine to overflowing, recalling the blessing of God's plenty, and breaks bread; dipping it in salt he prays "Blessed art thou, O Lord our God, King of the Universe, who bringest forth bread from the earth."

With the gift of worship that our numbers afford, we return to synagogue twice again on Saturday. In the morning I am honored to be asked to open the Ark and remove the sacred Torah for the Reading of the Law.

In the evening, the peace is shattered.

The Weill family picnics near their ancestors' home in Kippenheim, Germany: (from left) Bernard Max Weill, Violet Afriat Weill, Terry Weill, Geoffrey, Asher, and Judy Weill. Photo by Nathan Benn.

Suddenly in the midst of the prayers, we hear a crash at the synagogue door. A couple of the men leave their places and slip outside. After a time, they return and quietly rejoin the service. Later we learn that while we prayed, the doors of the synagogue had been stoned.

"Nothing new," our cousins explain with a shrug. "It happens all the time."

The next morning we stroll the narrow streets of the town, pausing for a moment before the old Afriat home, now a three-story hotel. Isaac finds us and takes us to say good-bye to two of our new Jewish friends, a seller of cloth in one of the town's many stall-sized shops and a plumber in a similar miniscule space.

They give us handshakes and smiles and a kind of touching gratitude for our having come. I can see them still, waving slowly as we disappear down the street, frozen in the isolation of a moment and a place.

Like so many other Mogador Jews, several of our cousins who had grown up in the Afriat home had gone to Casablanca to live. And there we found two, Doris and Vivienne Afriat, whose sisters Georgette, in Jerusalem, and Nora, in New York, we know well. These older women, who bear such a close family resemblance to my mother, have lived most of their lives in an apartment facing Casablanca's main street, the Boulevard Mohammed V, partly because of the memorial.

The memorial?

"It's here," Vivienne says, parting the curtain to the balcony and pointing to a hole in the outside wall. It was made by a shell fired by the Americans during the bombardment that preceded the Allied landing at Casablanca in 1942, beginning the African offensive.

"When the Americans marched in," says Vivienne, "we stood on the balcony and cheered as they paraded down the boulevard— the most thrilling moment of my life. Just the day before the Vichy

French here had ordered all Moroccan Jews to wear the Yellow Star."

Both fluent in English, Vivienne and Doris worked for the U.S. Army during the war and both won citations for their services. Out comes one of the faded, much prized documents. "To whom it may concern, Miss Vivienne Afriat has received official commendation and praise for outstanding performance of duty ... ." (signed) Irving O. Schaefer, Col. Infantry, Commanding North African Service Command.

"Father was so proud," says Vivienne. "He had no sons to win decorations."

As our Casablanca cousins live with memories in their twilight years, a younger Afriat cousin creates a memorable time in Marrakech. The wedding of Victor Afriat and Solange turns out to be the joyous highlight of our search for roots in Morocco.

At the small Marrakech synagogue, secluded behind a wall on a dead-end street, the couple—he in tuxedo and she in white lace bridal finery—meet under a green brocade chuppah, or marriage canopy, amid near pandemonium. The room is packed, with everyone standing and children climbing the posts to get a better view. After the wine is blessed, the women in the congregation loose a high, wild ululation—the North African cry of joy. The wine glass is broken, signifying the destruction of the Temple, and again the shrill trill comes. The marriage certificate is read and everyone bursts into singing. Men form a circle and dance. Suddenly the groom is hoisted to their shoulders. Then the bride. And the dancing and singing and laughter and cries go on. Finally, the bride and groom and wedding party march out to the strains of "Glory, Glory Hallelujah!"

At the wedding reception, in the blue mosaic courtyard of the Bahia Palace Restaurant, a seven-man orchestra plays without pause a night-long concert of Morroccan music, as first the young girls, then the women, then my mother—in an affirmation of her roots—take to the floor belly dancing. And on comes the wedding feast: almonds, walnuts, pecans, olives, pickled vegetables, peppered sausages, avocados stuffed with fish, cole slaw, tongue and capers, lamb and mushrooms, pigeons and prunes, hundreds of little cakes and candies, all washed down by Pepsi Cola, orange juice, mineral water, and Scotch whiskey.

It is a great festival, a togetherness, a happiness. At this moment, Moroccan and Jew are one in a felicitous meld of two cultures ... and so the pattern has been, with Jews holding fast to their own traditions even as they savor those of another people.

V
The Narrator Speaks

Jewish appreciation for the culture of a host country and the host's appreciation for Jewish culture reached its apogee during the 400 years the Moslems ruled Spain from the mid-eighth to the mid-twelfth centuries, known as the Golden Age.

Garnering wealth and influence, Jews became distinguished scholars and statesmen, poets and philosophers, financiers and scientists, helping to spark a renaissance in learning. Jewish linguists turned to translating into Hebrew and Latin the writings of the ancient Greeks and infused anew classical thought and ideas into Western civilization.

When Christian armies began the reconquest of Spain in the eleventh, twelfth, and thirteenth centuries, Jewish financiers and diplomats were often welcomed by Catholic rulers. By the late 1300s, however, hostility toward the ofttime wealthy and influential Jews had become widespread. Many, known as Marranos, took refuge in public conversion to Christianity while secretly adhering to Judaism. To the Roman Catholic Church, the Marranos were clearly the enemy and the Inquisition was established in 1478 to destroy them. In the ensuing investigations, Jews came under suspicion of helping Marranos and influencing them to hold fast to Judaic practices. Since the Inquisition could only act against professing Christians, professing Jews stood outside ecclesiastical control. But the situation was not temporal. King Ferdinand and Queen Isabella, in 1480, ordered all Jews to live apart from Christians, "hoping by their separation alone to remedy the evil," as they said.

Ultimately, they felt it was not enough. In the spring of 1492, at Passover, just after the monarchs had rid their lands of the Moors and united their kingdoms, their Edict of Expulsion fell like a guillotine on the neck of Spanish Jewry. After August 1492, no professing Jew lived in Spain for another 400 years.

Geoffrey Speaks

Jews are returning to Spain, the Edict of Expulsion having been formally abrogated in 1968, and now more than ten thousand make their home here, chiefly in Madrid, Barcelona, and the Costa del Sol. Among them are cousins on both our parents' sides. But we come to Spain not so much to seek out these relative newcomers as to walk onto a stage of history that saw the drama of our ancestral life unfold.

From our Tangier cousin, Lilian Marrache, we had learned that my great-grandmother, Rahma Toledano, was the daughter of Rabbi Isaac Toledano and a direct descendant of Daniel Ben Joseph Toledano, the celebrated rabbi of Toledo who fled during the expulsion, first to Salonica, Greece, then Fez, Morocco.

And so Toledo is our final Spanish destination, but in this month of March we start at Granada where, almost five hundred years ago in the same month, the beginning of the end befell Spanish Jewry.

We walk the gardens of the Alhambra, the magnificent palace begun in the eleventh century by Joseph Ibn Nagdela, the Jewish vizier to the Moslem Caliph Badia. Among majestic cypresses and the music of moving water coming from the snow-capped Sierra Nevadas on the horizon, we wonder: Did Queen Isabella and King Ferdinand, whose marriage was arranged by a Jewish diplomat, stroll these same paths, pondering the fate of a people whom they were reputedly disposed to favor?

Inside the Alhambra, whose splendor was said to have been inspired by biblical descriptions of King Solomon's palaces and temple, we seek the Courtyard of the Lions, where twelve life-size stone beasts, supporting a fountain, represent the twelve tribes of Israel.

Then, hand in hand, my mother and I enter the shadowy Hall of the Ambassadors, whose exquisite ceiling is cedar, inlaid with color: gold for riches, green for hope, red for God, and blue for heaven. And here in the Hall of the Ambassadors, the yearning of the human heart for riches and hope, God and heaven certainly found marvelous expression.

Here Queen Isabella heard the arguments of Christopher Columbus and, shortly, gave her support for his voyage of discovery, a voyage that would lead to the enrichment of her kingdom beyond all imagining.

And here the queen and her king signed the fateful Edict: "We command all Jews ... that ... they depart from all our said kingdoms and dominions ... and they shall not presume to return ... ."

And thus in 1492, night fell for the 150,000 Jews in Spain and, fittingly, it is dark when we reach Toledo.

Morning shows us that Toledo, Spain's medieval capital, built of yellow stone and wrapped in sunlight, is truly golden. Golden today, yesterday, and that far-off yesterday when in a spring as light and full of airs as our own, our Toledano ancestor heard the appalling news.

We visit today's meager remains of what they left: two preserved synagogues, the thirteenth-century Moorish-style Santa Maria La Blanca, which is now a church, and the fourteenth-century El Transito with gold brocaded walls and a women's gallery. We pause, as well, in the medieval mansion that had been the home of El Transito's builder, Samuel Levi Abulafia, the Jewish treasurer and confidant of King Pedro I of Castille. Two centuries later, the house had sheltered the master painter El Greco.

But it is in the narrow stone streets of the old Jewish Quarter, twelfth-century home of more than twelve thousand Jews, that imagination leads me to that other spring.

We do not know when our ancestor left Toledo, but as the city's rabbi the chances are that he stayed behind as long as possible to counsel and comfort those remaining until the last moment. Many would have left quickly after the news, knowing that the heat of summer, with temperatures of 100 degrees or more, could be killing on the road. Forbidden to "take away gold, silver, money, or other articles prohibited," as the Edict read, the outcasts sell homes, shops, and farms for horses and wagons and whatever they can transport.

In the sleepless night before setting out, they would have heard, as we did, the wind rushing down the canyons of the Tagus River in everlasting duet with water tugging at cascades of stone. And, come dawn, they would have bade those last agonizing farewells to friends and family remaining in the city.

The Jews most likely departed Toledo by the St. Martin Gate and Bridge, a span across the Tagus nearest to the Jewish Quarter and still standing, its great wooden door sheathed in hammered iron, its cobblestones rutted by the feet and wheels of centuries. Leaving the city by the bridge they faced—as did we walking in their footsteps—the same rock-bound heights known as the Cigarales, after the crickets that still sing there each summer night. Along the riverbank we glimpse the new green of willows, once the promise of rebirth in a Spanish land the Jews had known for 1,000 years. But then, no longer.

At the port of Palos during July of 1492 Christopher Columbus and his crews ready the *Niña,* the *Pinta,* and the *Santa Maria* for the voyage to what would be known as the New World. They could not have missed the gathering of the boat people, part of the Jewish refugees who, perforce, would sail forth to ultimately find homes in Turkey, North Africa, France, Holland, Italy, and other parts of Africa, Asia, and Europe.

VI
The Narrator Speaks

For a few, the flight from Spain ended in Germany and Eastern Europe, where the newcomers found succor among well-established Jewish communities. They were the inheritors of an earlier time when darkness fell over the continent of Europe following the fall of Rome in about A.D. 500. Then, the Jews found a special niche in society where they could perform a signal service.

Feudalism allowed only three classes—the nobles, the clergy, and the serfs—and locked each into its own sphere of activity. Agriculture and related activity being forbidden to them, trade and finance, including moneylending, were left to the Jews who, with their international connections with one another, were the only people in the restrictive society capable of thus serving the economy. And they became indispensable, especially to the rulers.

Furthermore, with the Talmud the Jews had an honorable and workable set of international laws to regulate their dealings, both among themselves and the gentiles. Living in relative freedom outside the feudal society, Jewish communities developed their own administrative councils, houses of worship, schools, public baths, burial societies, and social services for orphans and widows. With such organization, Jews found it desirable to live together in their own section of a town. Ultimately, the Jews of Europe were being forced to live apart from their Christian neighbors in what was called a ghetto, a word derived from the Venice neighborhood of Gheto, to which Jews were confined.

Those in Russia and the land that was historically known as Poland were confined to *shtetls* within the Pale of Settlements where, in isolation, the Jews were reduced to bare subsistence living. Many of the Jews of the *shtetl* embraced the Hasidic movement, a joyous form of Messianic Judaism with devoted adherents to this day, particularly in New York, several European cities, and Jerusalem.

When Napoleon declared the Emancipation that made Jews equal as citizens, many other nations in Europe followed France.

But not in the Pale, where frequent pogroms induced terror and prompted mass migration to America.

Even so, despite persecution the Ashkenazim of Eastern Europe grew strong in spirit and numbers. At the beginning of World War II, some three million dwelt in Poland; another three and a half million in Russia. Together they were the strongest force in world Jewry.

Asher Speaks

We go to Eastern Europe to walk in the footsteps of our rabbinical forebears who traveled between Germany, Prague, and Poland, caught up in the intellectual and cultural glory that made the Ashkenazim the major force in world Jewry from the fifteenth century onward.

But we go with mixed feelings, aware that the scythe of Hitler's Holocaust had destroyed the communities. What we are surprised to find, in Czechoslovakia and Poland, are the numbers of museums devoted to the Jewish people and their onetime life there.

Even more startling, we learn that the material for such museums was collected by the Nazis themselves, who were planning to transform the Prague ghetto and all the amassed Judaica into the "Museum of the Defunct Race." They lost the war before they managed to do so. The complex is now the State Jewish Museum, staffed by dedicated, enthusiastic non-Jews.

At the flamboyant Spanish Synagogue, the beauty of its wood paneling, painted in geometric designs, pales beside its contents: an incredible collection of some two thousand *parochot,* or Torah curtains, that once hung in front of Arks in synagogues across Europe. With brocade, velvet, lace, and embroidery in gold and silver thread, one curtain outshines another in richness and beauty, the oldest dating from 1592. We look in vain for the curtain looted from our Kippenheim synagogue.

The Meisel and Klaus Synagogues preserve the world's largest collection of silver Torah crowns, covers, breastplates, and pointers. Among architectural treasures the Pinkas Synagogue claims parts that are more than nine hundred years old, while the Altneushul (Old-New Synagogue), Europe's oldest functioning synagogue—and well known to our eighteenth-century ancestor Rabbi Nathanael Weil, who headed the most important Prague Yeshiva—still serves as a synagogue for the last remnant of the city's Jewry, some six hundred souls.

At eve-of-Sabbath prayers, I join a handful of frail old men, muffled in worn scarves, overcoats, and hats against the bitter chill of stone walls and benches, with the minyan completed only by a London salesman and an American student from Berlin.

At the onetime Jewish school, now the Library of the Jewish Museum, we make our silent way among the poems and drawings of children sent to the Theresienstadt concentration camp on their way to death at Auschwitz. "When the blossom comes to bloom," writes one, "the little boy will be no more." And another, with heartbreaking hope, "The time will come when we'll go home again." But the time never came for Petr Ginz, the brilliant fourteen-year-old student editor of a promising literary magazine, published secretly at Theresienstadt and now on display in the museum. He died at Auschwitz in 1944.

My great-aunt Bertha Weill Goldberg and her husband Karl, an Amsterdam physician, survived two years at Theresienstadt, the Nazi "model camp." A tall, imposing woman before the war, the small, shrunken Aunt Bertha that I met in 1947 showed the tragic cost of her ordeal. (Their son, Siggi, spent those four years in Amsterdam, hidden in a cupboard by a heroine of the Dutch resistance, Alice Koppel, whom he married after the war.) In a propaganda film called "A New Life for the Jews Under the Protection of the Third Reich," Theresienstadt is shown as having a bank, shops, cafes, kindergartens, and schools set amidst flower beds and good cheer. But beneath its cynical facade of normality there was incredible cruelty.

Walking around the village square, faced with stone and brick buildings and lined with elm, oak, and plane trees, we try to imagine the condition of life when, into this former garrison that had housed 3,700 people, the Nazis crammed 53,000 prisoners, where many, like the involuntary actors in the propaganda film, remained only briefly en route to Auschwitz.

But thousands died before deportation, and their bodies were burned in a crematorium that still stands in a grassy field dotted with symbolic stones for the nameless dead and memorials to each of the nations whose citizens lost their lives here.

We go to Lublin in Poland to see what might remain of the work of our learned cousins of the seventeenth century, Rabbi Jacob Ben Ephraim Naftali Hirsch, and his son, Abraham Joshua Heschel, whose research and teaching drew Jewish scholars from across Europe. And we find their legacy: An imposing six-story building of yellow stucco with white columns, dedicated in 1900, was once the famed Lublin Talmudic Academy that produced generations of scholars, teachers, and rabbis. It is now the Collegium Maius, part of the University of Lublin medical school.

On the site of Lublin's old Jewish market, now a park, we see a memorial marking the place where the Nazis set fire to a vast pyre of Jewish prayer books, ancient volumes of the Talmud, and the harvest of many lifetimes of Jewish learning, much of it known to my forebears. As the flames roared, the Nazis marched 125,000 of the Jews of Lublin and nearby towns from the square to the extermination camp of Maidanek, a few miles distant.

With the approach of the Red Army in July 24, 1944, a camp uprising prevented the Germans from destroying this extermination camp, and it was left, unlike others, virtually intact. And here it stands to this day, preserved as a monument to infamy. Row upon serried row of creosote-painted wooden huts stretch as far as the eye can see across the flat black plain, surrounded by a double row of high barbed-wire fencing, punctuated by wooden observation towers.

The afternoon is as gray and bitter cold as our mood when we arrive at the entrance to Maidanek and start up the road toward what appears to be a hill. But it is no hill. The elevation turns out to be a round granite dome, hanging above an enormous round granite bowl that is filled with something. From a walkway circling the bowl we look down on its contents. Gray ash flecked with bits of bone—human ash, human bone—and around the dome, the legend: "Let our fate be a warning to you."

The crematoria that reduced human bodies to ash are still intact, complete with dissection rooms to extract gold teeth and explore for other valuables that may have been swallowed. And the gas chambers that reduced human beings to bodies are still here too, built with an observation cell for SS troops to clock the speed of death, part of the first German experiments with Zyklon B gas. Here at Maidanek they found it to be the fast and efficient killer needed for Auschwitz and other death camps.

Our elderly guide, himself a onetime inmate of Maidanek, points out the deep scratches in the plastered walls of the gas chamber, torn by the victims in their last agony.

The human mind can only endure so much horror and I have had enough at Maidanek. But we must go to Auschwitz for Hugo.

Hugo was my great-uncle, a bachelor remembered by my father as warm and amusing. A native of Kippenheim, he was arrested by the Nazis at his home in Konstanz, Germany, on October 22, 1940, a member of the first deportation of German Jews organized by Adolf Eichmann as a pilot project, some 15 months before the infamous Wannsee Conference that decided upon extermination and "The Final Solution to the Jewish Question." Hugo was sent to Gurs, a concentration camp in the Pyrenees operated by the Vichy French, where he managed to survive the hard winter of 1941 when some eight hundred Jewish inmates died of "natural" causes. Twenty-seven were members of the Weill family.

The next summer, Hugo was transferred to Drancy, the main French transit camp near Paris, from which deportation of Jews "to the East" commenced on July 19, 1942. The Germans kept meticulous records. Hugo was part of Deportation Number 901/23, leaving Bourget-Drancy station at 8:55 A.M. on September 4, 1942. The deportation comprised 981 Jews in twenty-five railroad cars, under the command of SS Stabsfeldwebel Brand.

On September 6, 1942, Deportation 901/23 arrived at Auschwitz. The sixteen men selected for labor from Hugo's transport, plus twenty-one others, were given tatoo numbers 19170 and 19207. The rest went directly to the gas chambers, with fifty-seven-year-old Hugo among them.

The skies are spitting snow as I stand before the Auschwitz memorial and read the simple inscription: "Four million people suffered and died here at the hands of the Nazi murderers between the years 1940 and 1945." There is no mention that 90 percent of them were Jews.

Alone I stumble along one of the railroad sidings that had brought the deportation. Here it would be that camp doctor Joseph Mengele stood as a just-arrived line of prisoners files past and, with a flick of his whip, separates this man, this woman, those children into two groups, one for slave labor, the other for death.

Tears blur my sight and freeze on my cheeks.

VII
The Narrator Speaks

But there were always survivors. If no survivors of a single time and place, survivors nevertheless, in the larger sense whereby bits of Jewish life that had been blown to other parts of the globe in other times took root and grew. After 1492, Jews increasingly found haven in the New World, especially in the United States.

In fact, Jewish mathematicians, cartographers, and astronomers intellectually pioneered the voyages of discovery, and a Jewish map reader sailed with Christopher Columbus, who himself may have been a Marrano Jew.

The first Jews to come to what was to be the United States arrived in Holland's New Amsterdam from Brazil, after having backed the losers in a Portuguese-Dutch power struggle. When New Amsterdam became New York, the Dutch Jews became British colonials.

From the beginning, life for Jews in the United States was different from life as they had found it through long centuries in Europe, or, indeed, throughout time. And they were accepted, even assimilated, with little more than religion setting them apart. Why? First, Jews were no longer required to play middlemen in a society that had escaped constricting feudal traditions, and thus they could enter any trade or profession. Second, the Puritans and their spiritual heirs sought God in the Old Testament, just as did the Jews. Consequently, the wellsprings of the Jewish religion proved so nourishing that the Mosaic Code entered the American Constitution as a guiding force of democratic government.

Then came the greatest migration of Jews in their history, bigger than the Exodus from Egypt, or the Babylonian captivity, or the Expulsion from Spain. In the 1880s, some two million, mostly impoverished Jews from Eastern Europe—chiefly Russia—came on the crest of a tidal wave of emigration to the United States. To prepare the multitude for new lives, established Jewish communities set up vocational schools, hospitals, and other services, gleaning experiences of such value that they became blueprints for New Deal social legislation in the Depression.

Given their numbers, their innate abilities, their strong will to achieve, and the opportunity offered by a democratic system, American Jews have moved to the highest levels of success in such wide-ranging fields as government, academia, retailing, medicine, law, publishing, and the lively arts associated with moviemaking, broadcasting, and the theater. Indeed, they have reached the top levels in almost every field. With New York the largest Jewish city in the world and the United States counting more Jews than any other nation, including Israel, the Jewish Diaspora is, today, profoundly "Made in America."

Geoffrey Speaks

We stand, my cousin Peter and I, on the terrace of the Statue of Liberty and in the welcoming flood of spring sunshine look up at the immense figure lifting her lamp beside the "golden door." At the base of the statue are the words written in 1866 by American Jewish poet Emma Lazarus, "Give me your tired, your poor, your huddled masses, yearning to breathe free ... ."

"Yearning to breathe free ... ." That surely, as much as any single factor, has broadcasted the Jewish people across the earth and propelled them to the United States of America. I remember a luncheon conversation with the distinguished Rabbi Marc Tanenbaum, in which he said, "For Jews, the whole sense of the preciousness of life and their commitment to freedom and justice, America is the reincarnation of that ... supremely."

My cousin Peter—Peter Weill—comes to me from across half the earth, from Melbourne, Australia, the city to which his father, Hans Weill, fled just before Kristallnacht in Kippenheim, Germany. Peter—black beard, warm eyes, easy manner—is making his way around the world as a kind of finishing course to his university education.

Acting as his guide, I point to Miss Liberty, "This was the voyagers' first sight of their new Promised Land. Then their ships landed at Ellis Island." And from Ellis Island, most of those who entered the country moved into the tenements of New York's Lower East Side.

"One third of all the Jews of Eastern Europe came to the United States before World War I," I remark to Peter. "The Russian Jews were the *Luftmenschen,* literally, 'people made of air' whom the czars denied land and jobs and who, consequently, had to make a living out of thin air, so to speak. So they developed skills, such as needlework, and here in New York they provided the labor for the developing garment industry."

Unlike other immigrants, however, the Jews brought their intellectuals and, poor as they all were at first, everyone revered education and knew that it was their passport to a better future.

As we taxi our way across town, we pass the great department stores—Macy's, Gimbels, Bloomingdales, Saks Fifth Avenue—founded by Jewish merchants whose methods revolutionized retailing and created an American way of selling and buying recognized and emulated the world over.

Peter and I sit down to luncheon around the sculpture-graced pool in the Metropolitan Museum of Art, an institution infinitely enriched by the gifts of wealthy Jewish people. And then we stroll about to marvel at the ancient Egyptian Temple of Dendur, housed in the new glass-walled Sackler Wing, given by three Jewish physicians; to admire the fashions of the Habsburg era, an exhibition sponsored by the Edith C. Blum Foundation and seven of the great fashion houses of New York, five of them Jewish; and to feast on the masterpieces of paintings displayed in the Lehman Wing, the gift of Jewish brothers Robert and Philip Lehman, and the Andre Meyer Galleries, the philanthropy of another Jew.

Back for dinner at my home on the Upper West Side of Manhattan, Peter, my wife Terry, and I spread out on our apartment balcony overlooking Central Park and New York's mid-town skyline and watch the nightly spectacular when, with the flick of switches, the great city's skyscrapers burst into gleaming towers of light. Peter asks, "And you, Geoffrey—you and Terry—where do you fit between the immigrants of poverty and the princes of philanthropy?"

"Comfortably," I laugh, realizing that while there are still many poor Jews in the United States as well as a good number of rich and famous ones, Terry and I in our satisfactory middle class most surely represent the vast majority of the nation's 5.7 million Jews.

I arrived in America from England at age twenty-three as a travel agent for Thomas Cook & Sons and ultimately switched to my present position in travel public relations. Terry, a Weill cousin born in the United States, studied drama, then medicine, and is now practicing psychiatry in New York.

Our interests? Books, art, travel, theater, and relatives and friends with whom to discuss the above—over good food and drink. New York City suits us to perfection. It is a place where it is "normal" to be Jewish; where public schools close on Yom Kippur, the Jewish Day of Atonement; where parking restrictions are lifted on Rosh Hashanah, the Jewish New Year; where television announcers wish a "Happy Passover"; and where an enormous Chanukah candelabra lights up each December near the immense Christmas tree on Plaza Square.

Long before I arrived, New York had been hospitable to my family. My cousin, Walter Weil, came from Mannheim, Germany, in 1936 while another older cousin was forced out of Nazi Germany even earlier—Kurt Weill, the brilliant composer of "Three Penny Opera," "Knickerbocker Holiday," "Lost in the Stars," "Lady in the Dark," and other masterworks, left his native land in 1933 and soon settled in New York.

Two Kurt Weill revivals—"Rise and Fall of the City of Mahagonny" and "Silverlake"—draw Terry and me to Lincoln Center. Watching the "Silverlake" dress rehearsal, we are struck by the change-the-world idealism of the work; it was characteristic of Kurt Weill that he sought in the composition of music to affect social change. We go backstage to congratulate "Silverlake's" producer, Hal Prince, and its star, Joel Grey, both Jewish, and ask the question: "Why are Jews so prominent in the creative arts?"

"Respect for education," Prince replies without hesitation. "No matter how poor Jews are they respect education. And the arts follow education." And I wonder. Is it respect for education—for learning—that, in the end, ensured Jewish survival and, ultimately, attainment through the past and into the present? It is a question for a scholar and I seek out Rabbi Tanenbaum.

"Education, or learning, as the key to Jewish survival?" The rabbi considers the question. "Well, you may remember the command of Moses, 'Assemble the people, the men and the women

Asher Weill works at his desk as editor of Ariel, *Israel's leading cultural magazine.*

and the little ones, and the stranger that is within your gates, that they may hear, and that they may learn … .'"

"But it is *what* one learns," the rabbi continues, "that is important. Moses went on to say that everyone should learn the moral and spiritual teachings and duties of the Torah. It is to the glory of Moses that in a time when the best knowledge was usually treated as secret and reserved for the few that he inaugurated universal education of the entire People of Israel—as well as the stranger within the gates."

Rabbi Tanenbaum concludes, "But in the end, I think, it was the faith of the Jews, their religion, that ensured their survival."

And one last question. "Because they were God's Chosen People?"

And one last answer. "Our faith teaches that Jews were chosen not for privilege but for responsibility—a heavy burden, responsibility—to transmit to all mankind the eternal values that alone can save the race."

We gather, our family, Terry, and I, for Passover, the festival that celebrates rebirth, the Exodus from Egypt of the Children of Israel. Around our table we have drawn members of our far-flung family that are in New York. Cousin Norah Afriat, born in Morocco; Walter Weill, native of Germany; Peter Weill of Australia; my Aunt Ann Weill Storm, from England; and her American-born husband, Morry Storm, an upstate New Yorker.

We read together the "Hagaddah," which relates the familiar Old Testament story of the Children of Israel's last days and final night in ancient Egypt. As my forefathers, my grandfather, and my father before me, I explain the importance of special foods laid out on the Seder plate.

The Matzah, bread baked without leavening, to represent the rush of the Hebrew departure out of Egypt. The Haroset, a paste of apples, walnuts, cinnamon, and wine, representing the mortar used by the Hebrew slaves to build the Egyptian cities. Salt water, which symbolizes the tears of the slaves. The shank bone of a lamb, in memory of the Pascal Lamb eaten on the eve of the Exodus. A hard-cooked egg, whose shell is burned but not cracked, symbolizing the resilience of the Jews. And finally, a recent addition to the Seder plate, potato peelings that recall the starvation fare of countless Jews in Nazi concentration camps.

Scattered among the foods are other symbols, collected during our search for the family's roots. A piece of decorated plaster fallen from the roof of the ruined synagogue in Kippenheim. A stone from the cemetery at Oufran. A chip of broken tile from the synagogue floor at Mogador.

We taste each of the foods, one by one. And remember.

Out of memory come words that I glimpsed in a Fifth Avenue window of the Union of American Hebrew Congregations: "Passover, as a festival of freedom, is not only a memorial of liberation in times past but also the expression of hope for the day when all people, everywhere, will be free."

A Chosen People. Chosen for their responsibility to the world.

VIII
The Narrator Speaks

The coverage of the Jewish Diaspora was the crowning achievement of my career with the *National Geographic,* and the fact that it was never published was the greatest disappointment of my life. Why it failed to be published was never explained to my satisfaction. One reason cited was that the pictures depicted the tragedy of the Diaspora—concentration camps, ancient cemeteries, old men, former Jewish settlements in Poland—while my story showed the Jewish people in triumph, giving unmatched gifts to the world. Tragedies and triumph, true as they were, simply didn't mix, it was said.

But the story does not end with the failure to get it published for the millions who would have read it in the *National Geographic.* Much has changed since the early 1980s when the story was covered and written. The Weill brothers have lost their parents and other older relatives. Asher lost one of his two sons—the same that climbed to the top of Mt. Sinai with us—in a mountain climbing accident. But Geoffrey has gained a son and Asher has added two daughters to his family.

On the international scene, Jews are returning to Poland and Russia's Jews are permitted to leave at will, resulting in many coming to the United States. The struggle for peace between Israel and its Palestinian neighbors continues but with the active involvement of the U.S. government.

One thing does not change, however. The Jewish Diaspora gave me, personally, a once-in-a-lifetime spiritual adventure. What I learned about the Jewish people remains a living inspiration. As Max I. Dimont wrote in his book *Jews, God and History,* the Diaspora "… freed the Jews from time, from history and from death as a civilization. They had stumbled on the secret of eternal cultural youth." And I was privileged to share in that secret. With this book, I pray that you too will experience such an adventure in the realm of spirit, one that will excite and refresh you as much as it has for me.

Epilogue

"There are three things that last forever:
faith, hope and love; but the greatest of them is love."
—*The New English Bible,*
First Corinthians 13:13

*F*ROM THE BEGINNING THE DIFFERENCES between us were wide and varied. As mentioned earlier, I fell in love at first sight with airman Frederick Gillis Patterson, the manager of a Miami Beach hotel, run by the U.S. Air Force, where I was assigned by the American Red Cross during World War II. First difference: It took him three days to discover that he was in love with me, too.

But more seriously—and the second, more important, difference—Pat was from the top-class resort town of Castine, Maine, where his father was a lawyer, judge, and successful writer of novels. His mother was an intellectual and found her heart in great literature while tending to the myriad needs of her husband, children, and relatives. The family never felt the Depression of the 1930s and as members of the Castine Golf Club, situated on a height overlooking the bay and sea, they played the game with the rich and famous who summered in Castine. On the other hand, I grew up in Depression-afflicted Mississippi, realizing firsthand the terrible deprivations of that time.

Yet there was a third difference, born of the very circumstances of our youth. Judge Patterson was a Republican and a profound conservative in his personal life. He discouraged his sons—Pat's brother, Bill, was two years older—from driving the family car, fearing that they might have an accident. He did not encourage the boys to learn to swim, lest they drown. He even tried, unsuccessfully, to stop Pat from working as a caddy at the golf club, considering such activity demeaning for a son of his. In general, Pat followed his father in the fear of risk taking while I grew up

Mary Carolyn Bennett Patterson at her wedding in Kosciusko, Mississippi, October 28, 1945.

thinking that all risks were bound to improve my life. In the end, however, our differences made us a good match. Although a tiny bit late on his side, our love came to stay, through fifty-three years of ups and downs. His New England background added variety to my life, and my southern heritage gave spice to his. Pat's conservatism saved me from taking too many risks that might have proven a disaster. And though he never drove a car long enough to feel comfortable behind the wheel, thereby leaving the chauffeuring entirely to me, he became an almost perfect butler. I claimed that with our combined talents, we had the servant problem virtually licked.

Upon arriving in Washington, we fell into a wonderful round of social activity, joining the Mississippi and Maine state societies, mixing with congressmen on Capitol Hill, and making friends with Pat's Library of Congress colleagues and the journalists I met while working in musical public relations and covering the Hill for the *Cleveland News*. We added a whole group of new friends after I started work at the National Geographic Society, and they have remained with us for a lifetime.

But the desire to have children suddenly became overwhelming as I neared thirty years old. The National Geographic Society's policy about pregnancy was simple: The pregnant employee was required to resign after three months. The Society wanted no bulging stomachs or unexpected birthings in the corridors. So when I conceived Frederick Gillis Patterson, Jr., known from birth as Rick, it was "out the door" for me. Three months after Rick's birth, I asked for my old job back at Geographic—and got it. By then our situation at home had changed drastically, giving my career its chance.

Within the first month of our marriage, Pat's father died in an automobile accident, leaving his mother living alone in their large home in Castine. By the time Rick was born, Pat's mother, Bess, had sold the home and was living with her widowed sister, Grace, in Providence, Rhode Island. With the arrival of Rick, we moved Bess to Washington, to an apartment in the same building that we lived in. And it was she who took over caring for Rick during the hours of the day that I was at work. When Rick was four, we bought our large, Victorian home in the section of Washington known as Cleveland Park, and Bess moved with us into an apartment we created for her in the home. In time her sister joined her and we added a wing onto the house for the older women. By then we had our daughter, Lansdale Martyn Patterson, named after the last names of her two grandmothers and called

The author and her first-born son Frederick Gillis Patterson, Jr., called Rick, in his first year.

Landa. She arrived, incidentally, after I had won my campaign for maternity leave at the Geographic. Our three-generation household flourished. With a grandmother and great-aunt to watch over the young ones, we never had to hire a baby-sitter and I was free to travel. I had found one secret of having a marriage, children, *and* a career—wonderful, live-in inlaws. Another blessing, we had Grace with us until age ninety-five and Bess until age ninety-seven, both with sound minds and bodies fit until the end.

But there was another secret to my ability to reasonably combine marriage and children with a career. It was the personality and generosity of Pat, who through the years was my biggest booster, the man who thought I could do anything, who was always there to help cook, clean, or take care of kids, the ever-present help in times of trouble. Through the years, when speaking to college women, I have consistently preached: If you want a career with a satisfying marriage and fulfilling children, marry a man who wants it as much as you do and who is willing to match your 100 percent with his 100 percent. When you have it all, however, something has to give. During the years when our children were little, social life virtually went by the board. After jobs, home came first. Now they call it giving kids quality time. This is not to say that I did not feel guilty through the years, and often now, that I did not stay at home and oversee the young lives entrusted to us. Today, when either of our offspring suffers a failure, I blame myself for not building into them the prerequisites for success. But I am proud of them as the adult human beings they have become— intelligent, witty, full of high spirits and good humor—and I feel content with the job I did.

Of course, all did not go smoothly all the time in our three-generation home. While we had household cleaning help come in once a week, our loving older women did not feel they were doing enough to help out, especially when the children went off to school. Bess took over raking and weeding the lawn; Grace took over the laundry, manning the automatic washing and drying machines; both did dishes in the automatic dishwasher. They liked to make beds and sweep porches when needed. In the end they left us and the children few things to do around the home. Pat, at some stage of the game when Rick was about twelve, felt fatherly criticism rise at his son's nonperformance around the home. Calling Rick into conference, Pat said: "You know, Rick, you don't do very much around here. The children of the people I work with all have their little chores, mowing the lawn, bringing in wood, keeping up their rooms … ." The reply came back quickly: "Dad you are associating with the wrong kind of people." And the subject was closed. On another occasion, when Landa was about four and having trouble finding space in her bedroom for the more than 100 stuffed animals that she adored, Pat and Landa strolled over to the 10-cent store on Wisconsin Avenue near our house. As luck would have it Landa spied a stuffed animal she did not have and begged her father to buy it for her. "You have more stuffed animals than you know what to do with as it is, Landa. No, I won't buy you another." Nothing more was said until Landa and Pat returned home. At that point, Landa started stomping up the stairs to her room. "Where are you going, Landa?" Pat inquired.

"Up to my room to cry," came the reply, whereupon Pat returned to the store and bought the desired toy. We could rarely say no to either child. Tough love was an unknown thing in our family. And because Pat's mother and aunt were New Englanders with a built in quantity of reserve, they never voiced any criticism of our lack of child-raising skills.

Rick went on to Sidwell Friends School for nine years, then to Hawthorne, St. Albans, and Edmund Burke where he graduated. The University of Maine, American University, and the International School supplied his higher education. Thereafter he taught himself sound recording and became a freelancer, working primarily for Swiss TV as Independent Sound Services. He married a terrific young woman, Marlene Kress, who is some kind of computer whiz with an expertise I don't understand.

Son Rick and his bride Marlene Kress on their wedding day, June 29, 1991.

Daughter Lansdale Martyn Patterson, called Landa, and her daughter Bennett Bistline, named for her grandmother, in the summer of 1991.

Landa, seven years Rick's junior, attended the neighborhood's public school, John Eaton, before transferring to Maret School then Edmund Burke, where she graduated. She chose Kenyon in Ohio for her college and, upon graduating from there, married her fellow Kenyon graduate, Mark Bistline. They taught together in private schools in the United States and Britain before returning to St. George's School in Newport, Rhode Island. The marriage ended shortly after the arrival of their baby girl, named Bennett in my honor.

Pat retired from his government job in 1970, giving him the freedom to travel with me on various Geographic assignments. I retired from the Geographic in 1986 with a retirement party that sct a rccord for delight. At the time, the Society's Explorers' Hall featured a reflecting pool with a huge globe of the earth spinning at its center and fountains playing at both ends. At the party's climax, which took the Hawaiian luau as its theme, we all jumped into the pool and danced around the world.

Since my retirement, Pat—still my best friend and favorite traveling companion—and I set about seeing those parts of the world missed during Geographic years. I have lectured on cruises to Alaska, Portugal, around Africa, and across the Indian Ocean. We crossed South Africa on the Blue Train and camped out amid the animals of Botswana before going on to Victoria Falls. We barged down rivers in France and feasted on the beauty of great homes in Britain and Ireland. We went to Saudi Arabia to explore efforts to save a small antelope species, to Petra in Jordan to see for ourselves a poet's "rose-red city, half as old as time," and back to Israel to speak at a kibbutz. We walked the corridors of Cambodia's awesome Angkor Wat and toured Vietnam with our own van, chauffeur, and English-speaking guide. And finally, we returned to China to glimpse the great gorges of the Yangtze before they disappear underwater behind the greatest dam man has ever built.

On October 28, 1995, we received a group of fifty from the Cleveland Park Historical Society, who came to present a plaque declaring our home, at 100 years, the oldest in the area. Thereafter we poured champagne and opened the house for inspection. A few hours later, we were at the Cosmos Club, which had honored me with membership after the bar to women was dropped in the early 1990s. There Pat and I celebrated our fiftieth wedding anniversary with a tea dance.

With my sometime secretary and all-time helping hand, Evalina Busby, managing the affair and her musically talented husband, Stan, playing the dance music, we had a ball. Stan and his quartet even sang our song, "Laura."

At her retirement party from National Geographic, *Carolyn and friend, senior assistant editor Sam Matthews, dance around a spinning globe in the Society's reflecting pool. Photo by Joe Bailey.*

Near the end of the affair I made a little speech thanking the 200 guests—relatives, neighbors, and friends—for enriching our lives. They came from the National Geographic, the Society of American Travel Writers, the Society of Woman Geographers, the Wally Byam Foundation, and the St. Alban's Early Bird Swim Club. My old friend from Mississippi State, Joe Thompson, with his beautiful wife Jo, turned up along with two of the L.S.U. Owls, Che che and Jewel. My creative consultant, Martha Madden, flew in from New Orleans. And there was one hometown

Pat and Carolyn await guests for the celebration of their fiftieth wedding anniversary in the National Geographic Society Room at Washington's Cosmos Club. Carolyn was among the first women admitted to the club in the early 1990s.

voice from Kosciusko, Mississippi. When I learned that the Reverend Erskine Jackson, the Presbyterian minister who married us, could not come to the festivities, I asked him to tape the benediction he had spoken at the conclusion of our wedding. As a finale to our celebration, I played it for Pat and our guests:

> *"The Lord bless you, and keep you.*
> *The Lord make his face to shine upon you,*
> *And be gracious unto you.*
> *The Lord lift up his countenance upon you,*
> *And give you peace.*
> *Both now and ever more."*